DARREN CAMPBELL

TRACK RECORD

'I first met Darren when he was 14 years old and he had the ability to charm everyone he met and make them believe that he would be good at whatever he set his mind to. Over the years, I realised that there was a deep thinker behind that smile and the only person who could stop him achieving his goals was himself. At a time when Ron Roddan and I coached Darren, we were working with a hugely talented group of athletes who pushed, supported and motivated each other into achieving their goals and some of my proudest moments in athletics have been helping Darren achieve his dreams. He is family and always will be.'

Linford Christie OBE

DARREN CAMPBELL

TRACK RECORD

Darren Campbell
with Trystan Bevan

St David's Press
Cardiff

Published in Wales by St. David's Press, an imprint of

Ashley Drake Publishing Ltd
PO Box 733
Cardiff
CF14 7ZY

www.st-davids-press.wales

First Impression – 2020

ISBN
978 1902719 832

British Library Cataloguing-in-Publication Data.
A CIP catalogue for this book is available from the British Library.

Typeset by Prepress Plus, India (www.prepressplus.in)
Cover designed by the Welsh Books Council, Aberystwyth.
Cover image © Press Association

Contents

Acknowledgements

Thank you to all who have helped me along my journey, and to everyone who helped this book come to fruition, either directly or indirectly, in particular: Clair Campbell, Sophia Livert, Marva Campbell, Lynx, Mike Costello, Jo Osbourne, Sue Barrett, Marlon, Dalton Grant, Linford Christie, Darren Braithwaite, Paul Gray, Jamie Baulch, Malcolm Arnold, Daniel Plummer, Katharine Merry, the staff at Newport's Royal Gwent Hospital, Jason Gardener, Marlon Devonish, Mark Lewis-Francis, Colin Jackson, Anna Louise, Denise Lewis, Ashley Drake, Jill & Alun Wyn Bevan, the staff at Boston Tea Party and The One Elm (Stratford-Upon-Avon), Luke Bowen, Nick Walters, David & April Young, Steve & Susan Kaagan, Gemma Bonnett-Kolakowska, Rhuanedd Richards, Owen Martell, Lowri Roberts, Jon Williams.

Heartfelt thanks also go to the fans from all around the world who have supported me and continue to do so.

Preface

"Take it however you want."

From his answer to my question on a thorny issue in one of our first interviews, I knew Darren Campbell was one for straight-talking and not sugar-coating, for opinion not platitude.

We are all shaped by the people and places we bump into along the way and Darren's story is one of wading through adversity to create an indelible impact on his family, his friends and his sport. From the Racecourse Estate in Sale to the Hall of Fame in athletics, it's some journey – as compelling and inspiring as it is tempestuous.

A recent survey undertaken for the BBC revealed how modern audiences want to laugh and learn as they listen. For a decade and more, I've been laughing and learning along with Darren as part of the commentary team privileged to cover some of the greatest moments in athletics history.

His insights into the successes of Usain Bolt are unparalleled, delivered with infectious passion and underpinned by the credibility of his own achievements. The young buck who wandered into Sale Harriers at the age of eight has gone on to carve out success not only as a sprinter but also in coaching, broadcasting and in business, while taking significant chunks of time out to nurture the dreams of those who are next in line.

It takes a special character to yearn for more, to keep reaching out beyond the easy grasp and Darren has applied the attitude that brought him medals on the track to help fill the void that troubles so many when their days are no longer geared towards competition and the adrenaline and nerves have dried up.

Many of his experiences we wish we could have had, others we're glad we didn't.

Olympic gold and silver medals are but part of the story. Few of us can relate to the elation generated by the unforgettable sprint relay glory of Athens in 2004, just as the murder of a friend brings a darkness too scary for most of us to comprehend.

Some have been tempted to describe a dropped baton in a relay race as a tragedy. Darren Campbell knows better.

Mike Costello
June 2020

Foreword

The parallels between Darren's life and career and my own are numerous. Raised in single-parent families in suburban cities, our respective journeys to Olympic gold were characterised by our triumph over adversity, and by work ethic over endowment.

I first met Darren when he was a young athlete in 1988 and was struck by his raw natural talent as well as his presence: his posture and demeanour alone made it obvious he had already seen so much during his short life. We shared relatively similar upbringings, which almost certainly led to our friendship and mutual understanding that made us more than mere acquaintances on a track and field team.

Being an individual sport, athletics draws internal motivation and an inherent selfishness out of a person in order to be able to succeed but Darren was often gregarious and selfless to others, even as a youth. He was already on the path to success while also being respected and liked at the same time.

It was fantastic to be able to share my own Olympic triumph in Sydney with Darren's success at those Games, but our friendship was truly born four years earlier when I saw Darren at a crossroads in his career, and life, after the Atlanta Games. Out of love and respect for him as a person and his own ambitions, we fell out and did not speak to one another for well over a year. This person whom I had grown up with, and who was primed to take over Linford Christie's mantle in British sprinting, was in my opinion providing a disservice to himself and what he stood for. He was also abdicating an opportunity to provide a strong black male role model for those unable to see past the limits of their own social constraints. In knowing his background and his values, and the connection we had from our younger days, I am forever glad that he allowed me to be able to help him in whatever way I could.

Darren has always wanted to give to others more than he takes and, despite being an Olympic champion himself, he takes more pride in how he enables others to overachieve and succeed, through coaching, advising or mentoring. I have always respected his forthright views and his ability to articulate his sentiments clearly – aspects that were as prominent back in his junior sprinting days as they are now with his BBC broadcasting career.

Through the pages of his book Darren has provided more than just a highly readable account of his life and athletics career, he also gives a fascinating insight into him as a person, and has shared with us all how the many events in his celebrated life were shaped by a background that has created resilience and integrity, both on the track and off it.

Denise Lewis OBE
June 2020

Prologue

Running in the Wrong Direction

I could feel my heart in my throat. My mouth had long since gone dry and the late evening breeze and drizzle could do nothing to cool the inferno raging inside of me. The bright neon lights above made the sweat glisten on my forehead as my racing heart rate and stuttered breathing provided a harmonious fast-paced tempo. While rubbing the never ending sweat from my hands against my tracksuit, I realised that I was excited and ready. This was new territory for me. I stared down the narrow, dimly-lit lane, trying to block off the shouting and commotion of those around me. I took deep breaths. It was time to focus and to acknowledge what was about to happen.

I needed to be calm and control my emotions. I needed to project an aura of strength, power and authority. More importantly, for this to be a success I needed to instil such fear into others that they would not be able to react in time. The event itself might only last a matter of seconds but during those crucial moments, when others looked into my eyes, they would see a cold ruthlessness that would freeze them, motionless, to the spot. My success completely depended on it. I bit my lip hard, told myself to toughen up, narrowed my eyes, and decided that I was ready.

An instant hush descended as the moment approached. We looked at each other, analysing each other's posture, body language and demeanour for any sign of weakness that would betray inner doubts. We were, in truth, nothing more than a gang of young men, yet due to experience and circumstance we were all acutely aware that the next few minutes had the potential to change our lives forever.

This was it. We were set. To suggest that I could never have imagined in my wildest dreams that I would be here was an understatement. I didn't belong here, but fate had made up its mind.

There was one final rub of the hands to wipe away the sweat, and I pulled the hoodie over my head, tied the bandana around my neck and mouth, jumped on my bike and followed the others: I was on my way to my first pub robbery.

I was 16 years old, in a gang of six boys who were on their way to a pub in Manchester, and who shared the unspoken understanding that they were the crew who were going to rob it. We didn't know what to expect – most of us hadn't done anything like this before, and this would definitely be my first time. I was confident, verging on reckless, and yet I searched my inner self for any sign of doubt or uncertainty about what we were about to do.

I left little to chance in my preparation for a big race. This has a great irony, because were it not for an entirely fortuitous moment of chance I would almost certainly have found myself leading a life far removed from the one I have enjoyed thus far; and one where the running tracks and stadia of the world both as an athlete and commentator wouldn't have featured.

For, on the way to what would have been a misguided and juvenile act of serious criminality with severe consequences, that sign I had been looking for came. My bike suffered a puncture. I was held back. A flat tyre, of course, in the greater scheme of things shouldn't have provided a full stop, merely a comma, yet this moment is still frozen in my memory and I can transport myself there at any time. That feeling of, 'Why has this happened now?' consumed me. I know I had asked for a sign, but was this it?

This pause provided enough time for me to consider that it may have been, for me, preordained. I remember feeling at that time – as I do now – that there was a reason that my bike suffered a flat tyre, and that thought alone made me question the wisdom of going with the others. This didn't occur years later – the narrative entered my head as I was standing over the bike frame analysing the damage done to the wheel. A wave of clarity and a sense of responsibility hit me like a freight train. What would my mother think? What if something happens inside the pub that doesn't go according to plan? How have I found myself in this position in the first place? A 1,000-yard stare accompanied this inner soul-searching as the others waited to see what I was doing. This was all down an alleyway in Moss Side, under the glare of five of my peers who were ready to go and commit an illegal and dangerous act.

Luckily, my flat tyre had taken all of the momentum and aggression out of us as a group. Instead of us taking on the personas of reckless gangsters, brandishing weapons as we forced our way into a pub, a flat tyre on a teenager's bicycle suddenly brought into focus a comedic truth. We were just a bunch of idiotic kids about to wreck our lives, to act out the role we thought we were expected to perform, trying to emulate what our peers and elders had been doing for years. Suddenly, we realised were just six boys on bikes, not hardened gangsters. We could see ourselves for what we were.

The misfortune of a flat tyre suddenly became a fortuitous alibi. 'I didn't want to do it' became the more plausible 'I can't do it', and then 'I'm not doing this'. That journey of logic took all of ten seconds, and the butterfly effect that rippled from those short moments completely changed the course of my life.

This was an event borne out of the ecosystem in which it was created. A foolhardy notion such as robbing a pub was not an uncommon event at that time in that place. The only way kids from my area met lawyers was in court rooms – not at university, wine bars or networking events like the rest of society. It is said that the criminal commits the crime but society prepares the criminal: well, in this instance the only society that we knew had done its job all too well.

This might seem a lazy and tainted snapshot of the realities of inner-city Britain in the 1980s, yet all I can say is this – and there is no exaggeration or romanticising of criminality for effect behind these words – for me, there is nothing but shame and regret that I found myself in that position to start with. Life 'on the streets' has been glamourised excessively in music, television and Hollywood. A Scorsese film, a Channel Four documentary or a Dr Dre album gives us a hint of what it is like, within the context of the entertainment industry providing us with the shocks and thrills they know we desire. Real street life, though, is only attractive, if, at the end of it, you no longer have to live on those streets themselves. There is no glamour to be had living that life, it's all about those coming from there getting out and getting on to achieve better things.

And therein lies the problem. Street life as portrayed in film entertainment or music videos, or even in gritty inner-city documentaries and box set dramas was nothing like our lived experience. For us, life on the streets wasn't a late night, once a week hour-long episode, it was simply 'life'. It isn't a colourful and glitzy life when it is all you know and, more specifically, all that you believe you'll ever know. It builds an all-consuming 'thought-prison' of locked doors and high walls that are insurmountable.

We can all appreciate how this type of life can contribute towards a hardening of the soul, a sharpening of the wit and the drive of ambition; but what is absent from this well-meaning appreciation is the first-hand knowledge of its true and utter darkness. This life, for the vast majority, offers little but a black-hole, a vortex that sucks all hope and aspiration into its void. Most who are born there, die there, and so do their children. Social mobility does not exist on these streets, and this has not changed in 40 years, irrespective of which political party holds power. Many individuals try to effect change, but all those in power have all been equally guilty of neglect, abandonment and an immoral dereliction of their duty to help some of their own country's most needy people. Nothing has been done, certainly in my lifetime, to elevate street life from its position in society – at the bottom rung of the ladder. The sense of neglect and apathy has led to negative cycles repeating themselves too easily, and the tragic truth is that unless its people succeed in breaking out of the cycle, they inevitably find themselves contemplating breaking out of somewhere else instead.

The world will always seem a much harsher and crueller place to a boy from a difficult neighbourhood who grew up with nothing. When people abandon you, let you down, take things from you and leave you with nothing while showing not even an ounce of contrition, human nature will, more often than not, display suspicion before trust, and cynicism before faith. Yet despite this I have always attempted to rely on what I call my faith, and taken solace in attempting to see that disappointments or failures are often kinks in the road as opposed to the end of the road. My faith has always been a strong part of my life. Whether people call it faith, religion, spirituality, or give it another name, having a set of values anchored in the belief of 'doing the right thing', is important to me.

PROLOGUE

My faith matters because I have often felt a metaphorical guiding hand on my shoulder when forks have appeared in the road. Whether some attribute the puncture on the way to the pub that night as the hand of fate, or the work of God, that moment changed my life; of that, to me, there can be no doubt. While riding the bike with my friends from the estate that night I had neither the resistance to peer pressure nor the intrinsic maturity to make the right decision, and what might have occurred haunts me to this day and will do for the rest of my life. The fact that the only reason I did not commit a serious crime as a youth was because of an external mitigating factor, and not my own judgement, is a harrowing truth that I do not believe I will ever get over. As a father of three it is impossible to see my children grow without drawing the petrifying parallel of how I was living my life when I was their age.

I view the flat tyre in a similar vein to those other 'chance' occurrences in life that have far-reaching consequences; such as how one might view the moments that lead to a person meeting their life partner. These are moments forever etched into memory, where the fortune and blessing of the event is balanced with a sober realisation that it only occurred due to a culmination of a thousand variables, of which we were in control of none. The legendary Australian swimmer Ian Thorpe, who returned from the World Trade Centre back to his hotel having forgotten his camera on the morning of 11 September 2001 might empathise with me in respect of daring to think how things might have turned out. I looked at it as 'fate orchestrating our decisions' as opposed to 'decisions orchestrating our fate', and I can't think of a better explanation than that as to what faith means to me.

Do I look back at that incident, and maybe many others, with an element of shame? Of course, but I also feel a sense of bewilderment that something could have happened, at the critical time, which was so positive for me. Did fate intervene and prevent me from taking the wrong turn, or was it mere coincidence? I believe it was fate and, since that day, I have developed a strong faith and spirituality even though I've hardly ever gone to church. That experience also ensured I became a perfectionist. I vowed to never again depend on fate and that I needed to take control of my own life. I had been given a sign, and it was now up to me.

To Aaryn, Dillan, Leoni ...
... and Owen

1

Moss Side

"How can we stay out of trouble if we live here?"

Jesse Owens, one of the most famous athletes in history, was born on 12 September 1913. Exactly 60 years to that day, Darren Andrew Grant – the surname Campbell was to come later in my life – was born in St. Mary's Hospital, Manchester. To any black person, Jesse Owens ranks alongside Dr Martin Luther King, Nelson Mandela, Muhammad Ali and Rosa Parks as one of the greatest, most influential and celebrated black people in all of history. To be born on the same day as Owens became a touchstone for me. Such coincidences should mean absolutely nothing, whatsoever, in terms of life-plans and character formation, but to know that I share something, anything, with the most legendary sprinter of all time always brings a smile to my face.

Smiles on faces were plentiful and abundant during my childhood but, in truth, considering the circumstances and the environment in which we were raised, they shouldn't have been. I was born into a loving family but also into a desperate situation. Mum was on her own – my father had flown the nest before the eggs had hatched – and I had no father or father figure to speak of for a considerable amount of time. The nest itself was a small two-bedroomed flat in the middle of one of the UK's most deprived areas, the Sale Racecourse estate in Manchester. It was the kind of place where a family needed, above all else, a father figure for guidance and protection. We had neither.

Since then, having had a broad glimpse of how society operates and the norms we live by, I can now fully appreciate that we grew up in a state of poverty. Materialistically we had nothing, but our nothing was more than many others had who lived on the same street. We had very little indeed, surviving on hand-me-down clothes and borrowed furniture, and on the sliding scale of society's four tiers: abundance, sustenance, deprivation, and poverty, we were between the bottom two levels.

Living in poverty meant knowing, at a very early age, the difference between what you need and what you want. At Christmas we would get a single present and one year I remember getting a toy garage from my 'dad' (although in time I would come to know him as the person who I thought was my dad).

Our family unit consisted of my mum, Marva, my younger sister, Sophia, and me. Marva was born in Jamaica, and lived with her grandparents in the Hanover area of the island until the age of eight. In 1962 she moved to live with her parents in Manchester and was brought up on the Moss Side estate, where the very small number of black families, the new post-war generation of black immigrants to British shores, lived their lives within a fierce, insidious and heavily institutionalised racist society. A situation which was already logistically and emotionally challenging – living without her parents in the Caribbean and then moving over to a new country – was compounded by abuse, antagonism and hatred. By the time I was born in 1973, Marva had moved to the Sale Racecourse estate where her older sister lived. It was an area going through a significant social upheaval. The local council had moved a lot of the families from the most dilapidated buildings in Moss Side and relocated them to Sale Racecourse. At that time, the estate was not the kind of place you would choose to raise your family.

Mum worked all hours, in multiple jobs, just to keep the family fed and clothed. She sacrificed herself for us, and as children we were often looked after by babysitters or slept at the houses of friends and neighbours. The reality of living in poverty didn't just manifest itself through her endless struggle to provide for us, it was the constant moving of the goalposts that symbolised the simplicities of life. Poverty denied Mum the opportunity of spending time with her children due to the need to hold down several jobs in order to pay the bills. It also deprived us of her most valuable asset – her time. I'm sure she would have preferred to have come home at 5.30 pm, albeit exhausted, to her children – even if they needed to be fed, washed and put to bed – but poverty robbed her of these basic family norms. This was the very definition of 'just existing'. It was not what I now know as 'living'. Poverty equated to little idiosyncratic norms entering our lives that, to all other parts of society, would have been quirks, such as learning to appreciate when we had corned beef and rice for supper even though I detested it. It was better than the alternative, of nothing.

The greatest fraud that our poverty achieved, however, was in making us not feel poor. Because we experienced so little of what society had to offer, we didn't know what we didn't have. We grew accustomed to what we had, and were ignorant of what we didn't. I knew that some of my friends didn't get a meal every night, even though they would never admit it, so through knowing people who were worse off than us, we thought they were the ones living in poverty. I wonder if they felt the same towards people they might have known, who had even less.

Despite the obvious financial strains, I never felt disadvantaged. My mother took good care of us as a family and tried to ensure that we did not miss out, at least for some of the time. Sacrifices had to be made, of course, and when seeing the life and opportunities enjoyed by other families in school we came to understand that we could not have everything the way they did. Being a single mother to a family in a difficult and impoverished part of Manchester, which itself was devoid of economic investment during the 1980s, must have been a challenging task.

This state of deprivation even extended to our education. Because of the unsociable and unpredictable hours Mum had to work, she knew that she would not be able to pick us up from the school she wanted us to go to, so the options, both geographically and logistically, were limited. Ultimately, both my sister and I went to Princess Road Primary School in Moss Side, the school where most of our friends went.

From day one I was unsettled, and an insensitive decision by a teacher didn't help the situation. I remember there being three boys named Darren in my class and, because of this, one of the teachers – presumably to make their life easier – decided that I would instead be called by my middle name, Andrew. Immediately my life became a thousand times more confusing. Just at the time when I was trying to find my feet and establish my own identity in a new school, someone arbitrarily decided that Darren, from then on, would be Andrew. Having grown all too accustomed to being told what I could and couldn't have, to be told that I couldn't even use my name just added to my growing frustrations.

It was during a sports day at Princess Road school that Mum first saw me run competitively. I believe I was around five or maybe six years old and, despite the fact that I do not remember the race, she recalls that my abilities as a sprinter revealed themselves to her that afternoon. It persuaded her to enrol me at Sale Harriers for which, among many other things she did for me, I will be forever grateful. It is true that as a child I loved playing all sports, and of course being quick was something that was apparent to me at the time, but I equated that ability with being able to kick and chase past anyone while playing football as opposed to lining up on a track and sprinting between two white lines.

Mum tells me that I joined Sale Harriers as an eight-year-old. I cannot remember the chronology of it but I can vividly remember the experience. As is often the case with a person's first experience in unfamiliar surroundings, I can remember with great detail the scene as I arrived at the track for the very first time to register my name and begin training. I was a new member, which made me nervous, and I didn't know what lay ahead of me, which made me anxious. How would I perform in training? Would it be too tough? Would I be accepted? These were the emotions and thoughts that preoccupied me as I walked through the car park, over the fields and towards the track for the very first time. Yet my nerves and anxiety were about to be overshadowed by an event of genuine significance.

What is strongly embedded in my memory from that first evening happened as I was leaving the track. I noticed that many of my fellow athletes had both their Mum and Dad waiting in the car park to collect them. Two parental figures were there to greet them and enquire enthusiastically, as they climbed into the back seats of their cars, on how the night's training had gone. For me, it was just Mum, because there was no Dad in my life. The void created by the lack of a father figure had never been apparent to me before, and not being aware of it in the first place meant I was comforted by my ignorance. It just increased my appreciation of the work, and sacrifices, that Mum had made for us.

This seemingly innocuous scenario at the end of athletics training became a highly symbolic moment. I can still remember standing there and watching very normal family interactions that were so foreign to me. In truth, I initially struggled while attempting to compute and absorb what it all meant. My norms were different from theirs. I had no experience of having two parents collect me from anything, and I knew I never would. That realisation was something that would weigh heavily on my eight-year-old mind for some time to come.

The catch-all term of 'no-go area' is thrown around all too easily when describing run-down estates, but Sale Racecourse was so bad that it had its night-time bus services cancelled, so fearful were drivers of venturing there after dark. The *Manchester Evening News* described the estate as an 'island of deprivation in a sea of affluence', and this is as accurate a description as you could imagine. Greenery and beauty encircled our estate. Surrounded by the adjacent plush houses on The Avenue and the leafy suburbs of highly desirable districts nearby, we lived in the no-go area in the middle.

Poverty and crime went hand in hand, from petty theft to serious physical violence, and would occur so often that most crimes went unreported, but the area became infamous nationwide when shopkeeper Ian Marshall was shot dead in 1997 by two masked-raiders as he tried to protect his father-in-law. The murder shocked the surrounding area and the whole country, but for those of us who had lived there during the 1980s and '90s, this tragedy was merely a symptom of the decades-long malaise I'd grown up in the middle of.

As I progressed through primary school, the innocence and naivety of youth was slowly being replaced by a darker, more sinister, reality of what life in this area meant. The excitement of seeing police cars and ambulances, with their blaring sirens and flashing blue lights, was replaced by a growing realisation of why they were there in the first place. Because we were now going to bed later and spending more time outside of the house during the evenings, we began to witness more domestic arguments and violent street altercations. We also became more aware of the people and places to avoid. As we grew up, an increasingly brighter and harsher light illuminated our new world.

It wasn't just through the street life of Sale and Moss Side that we saw things change. School also became a territory of conflict. I, like thousands of others up and down the land, was bullied as a child. The impact of the bullying was twofold: firstly, the in-your-face, incessant targeting and name-calling whenever I came within sight of the bullies, and secondly, the lack of inner peace or sense of being secure. Whenever I was being bullied I was in fear, and when it wasn't happening I was in fear of being bullied. I was regularly beaten up by a gang of four or five boys. Not grievously, but often enough to cause ample emotional damage to a child as well as the occasional scrape and bruise. Being racially abused, of course, was a part of this, but that was such an ever-present occurrence and so self-evident as to almost merit non-inclusion.

The bullying continued into high school. Being the only black pupil in a school year of approximately 250 children in Ashton-on-Mersey, I was used to being conspicuous because of the colour of my skin, yet I quickly noticed that the racism I experienced was inflicted by the same characters who also felt the need to undermine the confidence and strength of other pupils, for other reasons. It eventually clicked with me that this was because they lacked confidence or felt inadequate for some reason themselves. It's telling how that always seems to be the case with bullies.

Mum only became aware of something not being quite right because, in her words, she noticed that I'd started walking around with my head slightly tilted. Being bullied affects many people in many different ways, and the solution as to how society eradicates such a toxic problem is for minds greater than mine to address, yet in time I felt that it transposed a negative energy and swagger onto me that, ironically, became similar to that exhibited by bullies themselves. The posturing and the feeling of a burden of weight on my shoulders was a coping mechanism in an attempt to project strength when, in fact, any confidence and strength I had was being eroded, bit by bit, on a daily basis. I am convinced that people considered me arrogant, hard to approach and aloof when, in fact, I was meek, desperate for closeness, and actually a little bit shy. Bullying ensured that I built walls around myself in order to ensure nobody got close enough to hurt me.

I would like to claim that the bullying gave me focus, emotional strength and the drive to show the world that I was an ambitious achiever, and that it spurned me on to greater things. However, the final act to this particular story occurred strikingly early. An early adolescent growth spurt meant that by the age of 12, and just before I finished my first year at Ashton-on-Mersey, I had grown to 5ft 8ins of solid muscle, with size 11 feet. I found myself towering over my peers and that physical stature gave me a growing sense of confidence and strength. By now the bullies weren't so keen to enforce their malevolence onto me. Suddenly I wasn't being bullied and, more importantly, I realised I couldn't and wouldn't be bullied either. The realisation that my growing physical strength was the reason the bullies were now backing off helped me understand that they were, indeed, cowards masquerading as tough guys.

Unfortunately for that gang of bully boys, the experiences of being bullied I'd endured were raw enough to leave a very bitter taste in my mouth, and left a burning and overwhelming desire for retribution. This was an itch that needed scratching. I hate to say it, for it reduces me to their level, but they had it coming. I beat them up. Not enough to cause real harm, but to ensure that they realised every action merited an equal and opposite reaction. I would like to think, at the very least, that I taught them the notion of cause and effect.

The experience taught me the value of projecting brute strength over the societal ecosystem in which I was brought up. "Leave me the fuck alone, and everyone will be ok" became my mantra.

Mum showed tremendous fortitude and determination with both Sophia and me during our school years. Despite her insistence that I was as intelligent as Sophia – in truth I was too lazy and distracted to apply myself – she not only took it upon herself to enrol me with Sale Harriers to nurture my talent for running. She also knocked on endless doors in order to get Sophia an assisted education by accessing the funding and support she would not have been able to afford. She applied to charities and to various foundations, and by sheer chance discovered a wonderful lady called Margaret Harrison who worked in an office next door to her. Margaret had experience in private school funding and, through the goodness of her heart, she pointed Mum in the right direction.

Sophia was an academically gifted child, but in order to flourish and achieve her full potential she needed additional support. Mum knew that her long working hours, combined with the logistical juggling to enable my extensive athletics commitments, meant that this support was impossible so she devised an alternative path for Sophia: private education. Through the Family Welfare Association, Mum managed to plead her case successfully and the seed was sown, not only for Sophia's education, but also for Mum to be able to ferry me around for my athletics. Back in those days there was no lottery funding for athletes or coaches, and there were no bursaries for talented sportspeople. You had to carve out your own path and if societal barriers got in the way, your road to success was blocked. Mum simply refused to allow our family circumstances to block our progression and found herself continuously spinning plates to keep her wishes for us on track. With Sophia being so studious and academically minded, it became apparent that sport might be my outlet as much as academia would be Sophia's.

Mum's determination, Sophia's academic traits, and the invaluable advice of Margaret Harrison facilitated my sister's educational progress and, as a consequence, my athletic development. It was the perfect outcome for us both, but we still had to work hard to make the most of this opportunity. Sophia's personal sacrifices, in order to attend the prestigious Stockport Grammar School, included having to take a bus from our estate to the middle of Manchester, and then another one on to Stockport every morning and the same journey back every evening.

Ashton-on-Mersey School was where I met Denis Law. His name was actually Dave Law, but seeing the name Mr D. Law and the subliminal effect of being a Manchester kid, there was no other option than to presume he was the Scottish football icon. I was the only black student in my entire school year, and there were another three or four more in the fifth and sixth years. We were naturally drawn to each other and because of this I got to know some of the pupils in those older age groups more than my own, and they also looked after me. Because of the socio-economic catchment area of Ashton-on-Mersey, I also started to mix more with children who were not from council estates. This was a new experience for me. The school had a mix of council estate kids and those who could be deemed as privileged kids, so the wider spectrum of society revealed itself to me for the first time.

By the end of my first year in secondary school, I had firmly cemented myself in the bottom group for every single subject. I was a typical low achiever and was both disruptive and frustrated with the educational system. There was always an academic side to me – chess was one of my passions while at school – but the application to learn was missing. This was also the time when I began to get bullied, so for educational and emotional reasons my experience of secondary school was an exceptionally unhappy one. I was an angry kid, noted for daydreaming and shunning work, and when summer came at the end of the first year, I was desperate for the six-week break.

This was the summer of 1984. The summer of the Los Angeles Olympic Games, the summer of Ed Moses, Evelyn Ashford, Saïd Aouita and Daley Thompson, and most of all it was the summer of Carl Lewis. This was when track and field played its serendipitous part in my life. I was at an age, and at a time in my personal development, where things were so bleak and desperate that I was very receptive to any positivity and encouragement. Carl Lewis, the all-American hero, was about to emulate the great Jesse Owens – the icon with whom I shared a birthday – in winning four gold medals: the 100m, the long jump, the 200m and the 4 x 100m relay. I was glued to the television. I watched every race, every heat, and Lewis – in becoming the new Jesse Owens for a younger generation – instantly became my idol. The glamour of those Games, transmitted through our televisions with the yellow tint of Californian sunshine, became the theme of the summer and Des Lynam's distinctive voice became the soundtrack of my summer mornings. It was wonderful. I was teleported to another life, a happy life, one where I was beaming from ear-to-ear. I said to myself there and then: 'I want to do THAT'.

Returning to school that autumn, I couldn't keep my mouth shut, to pupils and teachers alike. The LA Olympics had inspired me. They had awakened a part of my soul that I didn't even know existed. I proudly announced, aged 12, to anyone who would listen, that I was going to be an Olympic athlete. But I was ridiculed. I was told to stop daydreaming. Most of the teachers were either dismissive or, in one instance, aggressively contemptuous. I was told from by one that most people from my area who held those kinds of pipe-dreams ended up in prison or dead. I was dumbfounded. I had discovered something which had given me inspiration, joy and purpose, and I was now being derided by those same people who held the keys to my future. The result of this was obvious. I became more and more disruptive.

Not only was I being bullied, ridiculed and marginalised academically, down to the very bottom, but the one thing that gave me joy, hope and inspiration was being scoffed at. The teachers became as alien to me as the bullies, except for two of them – the aforementioned Mr Law, and Mr McGowan.

Those two teachers gave me the hope I needed. The pair of them were totally supportive of my new-found enthusiasm. Maybe it was because I had found something to actually be enthusiastic about. They also suggested, very persuasively, that I needn't worry too much about the opinions of the other teachers and pupils, for if I truly wanted to be an Olympic athlete, they saw no reason why I shouldn't be. Mr Law was the arm around the shoulder that I needed at that time. Freud would have a field day with this scenario. Here I was, an angry and bitter young man from a one-parent family and with no father figure, being supported emotionally by senior male figures in a powerful and influential way. Mr Law and Mr McGowan were also powerful, physically, and were very masculine men. They oozed gravitas and had an aura about them that earned my respect. From the moment they supported my dreams – unlike the others – those dreams became possible for that 12-year-old pupil at Ashton-on-Mersey School. I can never thank them enough for it.

Academically, I still had a problem. I was still disruptive and a pain to most teachers, and I was still badly underperforming. In my view, the teachers hadn't supported my will and ambition so why should I support theirs. They had ridiculed me and didn't engage with my needs so why should I reciprocate? My interest in sport was blooming, but it didn't disrupt my academic progress as there was no progress to speak of in the first place.

My mother cannily used my sporting obsession as leverage. I was banned from all sports, then given a choice. Should I decide to work hard, improve my academic performance and personal attitude, the sporting outlet would be reinstated without delay. This ultimatum made an immediate impact, not only on my teachers, but on me. I made the decision to work hard and, almost overnight, everything turned a sharp corner. Even the teachers' attitude towards me changed when they saw the dramatic improvement in my behaviour and attitude. A positive cycle began, where encouragement led to hard work which led to improved grades. I even moved my seating positions in the class from the back to the middle, and ultimately to the front. My mum had played a masterstroke.

I do remember one incident, however, where I was in a maths class with Mr McGowan and the disruptive genie came out of the bottle. How or why I was playing up I cannot recall, but I clearly remember the words said to me by Mr McGowan: "You want to be an Olympic runner, your dream is set and we all want you to succeed at that. The problem here is the other 29 people in this class. They might not yet know what they want to be, but you are ruining their chances of discovering their own dreams."

This softly spoken dressing down from a dominant male hit me like a lead weight. It might have been due to the previous lack of a father figure showing me the way, but I was in desperate need for positive male influences to illuminate a path for me, and after this incident I don't believe I was a problem for a single teacher thereafter.

Mr Law always encouraged me. He tried to understand me and inspire me and give me wisdom to achieve my goals. He also fought for me to compete in an international championship in Brugge, Belgium, during an exam period, and facilitated this by allowing me to sit the exam out of hours with him invigilating. Mr Law made it possible for people like me to dream big.

I loved athletics but, one huge dream of mine was to play football for Manchester United. Thanks to adolescence, and its gift of giving me speed and strength, I was soon the proverbial 'boy in a man's body' when it came to sport, and I became relatively talented at football. As a result, someone recommended me to the Trafford School of Excellence which, in those days, was a breeding ground for those who would end up playing at Old Trafford. However, once at the School of Excellence I quickly came to appreciate the gulf in standard between those who were 'relatively talented' are those who were 'truly gifted'. Luckily, that acknowledgement, rather than destroying my confidence, drove me closer to athletics much sooner than chasing any football dream through delusion might have allowed. The true reality check of any football ambition was confirmed to me by the presence of one player. There was a boy called Ryan Wilson in the same group as me. He was phenomenal. He could run almost as quickly as I could, but with the ball at his feet as if it was super-glued to the outside of his boot. In games he would often score a hatful of goals, well into the double figures, and would make very good players look clumsy. Even at that age it was blindingly obvious that, given the correct guidance, this boy was going to play at the top level. I remember watching him from afar, smiling and thinking, 'I am on the same pitch as someone who is truly blessed'. To this day, Ryan Wilson is mentioned in the same breath as George Best as one of the best footballers to have never played at a World Cup. Most people of course know Ryan from his mother's surname which he adopted later in life – Giggs.

Outside of school, my social life was progressing on the Sale Racecourse estate. I was hanging around with most of the same friends, and we were experiencing all that the area had to offer us. The tiny number of black kids at Ashton-on-Mersey, and the reality of our situation that saw us form a tight-knit group meant that a gang mentality was already starting to form. My name, to those who knew me, was 'D' or 'DC'. A few other black kids now went to the school, including Lynx, Tommy, Ashley and Marlon, while in the year above me there was 'Trevor', and in the year below there was 'S'. This is how our little crew got formed, all known by our nicknames, and none ever known by our Christian names ever again, except by those who didn't know us.

Marlon had moved to our school when his family relocated from Hulme to Sale. The racism he encountered in Sale and at our school was a shock to him. It was far worse than he'd previously experienced. The new reality for him – which was already a norm for us – was the daily fighting, name calling, and threats. He immediately joined our tight-knit circle which got even tighter with each incident of racism. We were all talented sportsmen, whether athletics, basketball or football and we were all good kids, but the problem for all groups of teenagers was that the 'wrong crowd' was always just one person away, and Marlon, slowly but surely, slipped down the slope into associating with the wrong crowd. As drugs took a firmer grip on society it was inevitable that the kids who'd been the schoolyard hustlers, selling chocolate and other sought after treats, were drawn into dealing much more serious, and deadly, products.

There was a black kid in a grammar school we had to walk past to get to Ashton-on-Mersey. He was the only black kid in the entire school and we made it our job to ensure that he didn't get messed about. This further nurtured the development of what society would perceive as a gang mentality. With it, the protective nature of looking after one another, and selected others, led to us to adopt an aggression which was the final pretext to a gang manifesting itself.

At the same time our Sale Racecourse crew was drawing tighter and more gang-like, because of my interest in athletics with Sale Harriers, my social circle expanded to include new friends from a wider social base. Track and field is celebrated as being a sport where the appreciation of the effort and discipline of others is often rewarded with respect, and this respect crossed all geographical boundaries outside the estate. I came to know other people from other gangs because of this, and in an affable and amenable way. Whatever friction or rivalries that existed between groups of people on the estate, this 'other' circle of track and field friends – who came from multiple gangs – developed social interactions on the street, of head nods and handshakes, where previously there might have been territorial belligerence and awkwardness. When you combined, "He's okay. He's with me", with, "He's okay. I know him from track", the net of personal safety widened considerably. We joked that we had the 'freedom of Manchester' in a safety sense – a joke which itself illustrates the fact that we weren't used to having things that people in other parts of society took for granted. Everyone has the freedom of their own town, yet for us growing up in Moss Side and the Sale Racecourse estate we were made to feel as if we didn't.

During this period, the familiarity of spending time with friends, combined with knowing who your friends actually were, led to lifelong alliances with special people. One of whom was a cheeky character we called Lynx. The concept of pseudonyms replacing actual names would be familiar to anyone growing up on those estates, and once names were adopted there was no going back. It would also be both peculiar and disingenuous for me to use names here that, in truth, I haven't been using for the best part of 40 years. Lynx also grew up in Sale, and we have known, helped and looked after each other, in equal measure, for over four decades. We also shared a similar back story insomuch that his dad had left home when Lynx was around three years old to return to Jamaica. He once confided to me of his heart-breaking realisation that he couldn't remember if he recognised his dad's face from either seeing him in the flesh or from photographs.

Lynx was a few years younger than the rest of us and, having that same father-shaped hole in his life, was in the need of male role models.

As a crew of friends, and with him being the youngest, we felt a duty of care towards him. Also, from a perception point of view, how people treated him became a proxy litmus test for how we were respected as a gang. He had our protection, and if he was left alone, that meant that we were well regarded, or at least acknowledged. The problem was, though, being the beneficiary of this kind of protection and safety resulted in us inadvertently unleashing the beast within Lynx. The self-assuredness that we gave him grew into an overt confidence, and when he saw the anger and violence that was all around, it became a dangerous mix.

With the gang now fully functional, Marva now assumed the role of the disciplinarian for us all. She would often drive around the estate to check that we weren't up to no good, and the sight of her in her car became more of a reason to hide and dive for cover than if a police car had driven past. The mums of all our crew knew their sons were afraid of her, so being 'out with Darren' became a licence to stay out later as the mums thought we wouldn't dare misbehave, fearful of Marva's wrath.

We were not a troublesome crew, particularly compared to other gangs in the area earning thousands of pounds per day through crime. We were more interested in staying out of trouble than creating it. Also, maybe because of our harmless nature, we had a wide network of friends that extended outside of the estate through which Lynx soon recognised there was more to life than Sale. We expanded his horizons. Because of this dynamic, he and I began to disagree. He felt that in searching for new friends and experiences outside of where we lived, we were ultimately destined to leave him behind. He saw this as a threat, as we had only recently developed into trusted role models for him, and losing this was the last thing he needed. This led to arguments and we got into a few altercations, including throwing punches and threatening one another.

Surrounded by violence, what we really needed from each other was friendship. The crime statistics of Moss Side and Sale Racecourse in the late 1980s and early '90s painted their own picture. There were hundreds of shootings every year, many of which involved territorial enforcement, with many of them creating casualties and sometimes fatalities. The city's nickname of 'Gunchester' told its own story. One of the greatest contradictions was that we felt the police presence didn't protect us from harm or envelope the community like a warm safety blanket, as it would in other neighbourhoods. As a young black man I could still find myself, while driving a car at night, being pulled over three or four times just so the police could be assured that, 'everything was as it should be'.

Our interaction with the police, as a community of young men, became a metaphor for communication. We learned that if you ran as soon as you heard the sirens, the police's perception was that running signalled guilt. The only people who ran were the ones who had done something to merit running away from the police. Ironically, for a sprinter, living under such conditions taught me the value of *not* running. There was no point escalating any incident or situation through not communicating and simply running, as it only lead to mistrust and suspicion, so we learned that if you engaged with people instead it created an aura of calmness and a perception of innocence.

Through this, Lynx and I learned the value of composure in the face of adversity. When he was younger and smaller he needed our protection yet, as he grew physically larger and more confident, we needed to protect him from himself in a tinderbox-like environment which only needed a small spark to create an inferno. He developed the ability of using kind, calming words effectively, because everyone knew it was always backed up with a muscular growl should that become necessary. The threat of physical violence to stand one's ground was never far away on those streets, so having someone with that ability in our group to diffuse, as well as intimidate, proved invaluable. He also developed an intelligence which, for us, made intelligence desirable and therefore aspirational. He had the valuable ability of making others fearful that a beating was coming, but then thankful when it didn't. The reason that he brought that fear in the first place, however, was that if pushed to a place where the calmness and wisdom dissipated, anyone that got in his way would instantly regret it. Having Lynx play such a central part in our lives proved fateful for us all, and would prove to be life changing for me later on in my athletics career and beyond.

Growing up in this area was akin to standing in quicksand. With each passing moment its grip on us tightened and the longer we stayed within its influence, the lesser the chance that we were ever going to free ourselves of its stranglehold. Having been born into a grey concrete existence dominated by crime and injustice, and once I acknowledged the wider palette of colours and a kaleidoscope of experiences that the outside world provided, my outlook changed remarkably. It brought happiness and a sense of potential that I was previously unaware of.

This is how my Moss Side upbringing has made me more positive and more inspired. The parameters within which I existed, however, meant that a day without aggression or intimidation was one that brought peace of mind. Aspects of life that people outside places like Moss Side would not need to give a second thought to can affect lives on a daily basis within those communities. Yet as kids we weren't acutely aware of this. We felt that we were the same as all the other kids growing up throughout Britain. We were immersed in school life, in our family's realities, and we lived through the interactions we had with our friends. We weren't aware of our own levels of deprivation or poverty (that was to come later), and on weekdays we got through school in order to play with friends on weekends. When it is explained like that it seems so normal.

There were gangs on the estate that overtly made money from theft and dealing in stolen goods, which resulted in there not being many positive male role models for us, especially with absent fathers being a recurring theme. By the age of 18, I had known numerous people who had gone to prison, countless properties robbed in our vicinity, continuous gangland violence and the presence of drugs all around us. Murder, crime and poverty were themes that I only became aware of as being abnormal when I realised that they were things most people didn't experience in their daily lives – that's how accustomed to it all we became. We were good kids, slowly being shaped into a gang of ne'er-do-wells, but the mantra we lived by was simple: "How can we stay out of trouble if we live *here?*"

2

Sale Racecourse

"Can you leave Manchester now please Darren?"

By my mid-teenage years, our group of friends had now solidified into a 'gang'. We were young black men, looking out for one another, and also looking out for other young black men in the neighbourhood. We took part in all the normal activities of playing football, going to community centres, playing on the streets, and hanging out outside shops, but we were identified by the fact that we were a close-knit group of friends who trusted ourselves and nobody else. Our goal was simple: we just wanted to make some money. Had we been a group of middle-class white guys living in leafy suburbia, we would have been labelled young entrepreneurs, but we were black Moss Side boys so, of course, we were labelled as a gang.

Some of our more 'entrepreneurial' initiatives involved such lowbrow dealings as selling the dinner tickets we received from school. Most of us got free meals so we would sell the tickets, share the money between us and sometimes treat ourselves to a KFC instead of having school dinners. Someone, somehow, managed to source some mobile phones for us at a time when, back in the early '90s, such things were bricks normally used by upwardly mobile New York yuppie types or inner-city drug dealers. We were aiming for the former, in order to escape the latter. Our crew were interested in hustling, and making money. The ability to hustle well was a gift, but also a curse. The temptation to over-step the mark into illegality was huge because when we looked around us, everyone was making far more money than we could fathom.

Marlon was getting deeper into the wrong crowd from further afield after spending more time in Moss Side, and was becoming a bridge between our crew and slightly more infamous personalities that had a habit of crossing the line. Marlon had never taken drugs in his life but was now firmly on a path to where he would be reprimanded several times and sentenced to periods in prison on more than one occasion. Even as young teenagers, we heard that the police had already given us a moniker: the NFH - 'The N*****s from Haydock'. Moss Side was brewing to be one of the worst areas in the country for gun crime and drugs, and we were inadvertently being dragged into the middle of it, due to simple geography and personal association.

Despite the gang bravado growing within us, the biggest thing we all feared was the disapproval of our mothers. I respected my mum for how she had taken on the desperate situation she had found herself in, but I also feared her. The form the fear took also changed as I got older. I was initially afraid of getting a clip around the ear, or a good shake, for any wrongdoings. Mum was a strict disciplinarian which, thankfully, played a strong part in keeping me from falling in with the wrong crowd. The influence she had over us as children played no small part in our being able to recognise right from wrong, but also between what would get us employed and what would get us shot. My world revolved around my mum. Having already experienced the hardships of living without her parents in Jamaica, and struggling with deprivation after moving to Manchester, her influence on me was huge and she was the source of my values and morals, without which who knows what would have happened to me.

Being a typical teenager, I was the one who was always right and Mum had no idea what she was talking about. How could she know what life was like for a rough estate kid trying to make his way through life? Of course, in time and with experience I became afraid of her being right all of the time. The things she was limiting us to, and warning us about, had a nasty habit of happening to somebody else, often with dire consequences. The rules and boundaries regarding what we couldn't do were always firmly set, and the worst thing in the world was doing something which ended up proving Mum right. This would be the end of the world for a young boy looking to gain respect in society, and wanting to be perceived as being mature enough to make his own decisions. Messing up and having the 'I told you so' dressing down became the ultimate deterrent.

In the end, as I think we all do, I reached the level where I simply didn't want to disappoint her. I wanted Mum to be proud of me. I never was the kind to indulge in smoking or drinking purely in order to be rebellious – not only because in Moss Side that level of rebelliousness didn't even register as a blip on the radar compared to the theft and vandalism all around us – and because I simply didn't want to let her down. It is fair to say, therefore, that in hiding my misdemeanours from Mum, or coping with the discipline when I did get caught, she inadvertently made me physically tough, wise, cunning and, hopefully, proud.

The feeling of not having any real control over our own destiny was one that was thrust upon us as a family. People don't have the choice of whether they are born rich or poor, but having even a modest amount of money allows families to exert a certain amount of control over their lives. Money enables choice, and that can't be realised until you don't have any of either. The situation in which our family found itself, in Manchester in the 1980s, was one rooted in that lack of control over our own destiny. My mother only told me later in life how close to the bone, financially, we were at certain points, and maybe in light of this I was wholly determined to show that a child from a single parent family from a council estate in Manchester could turn himself into a success. I had seen many people from the estate who had either gone to jail or suffered an even worse fate and, often, these weren't bad people but characters painted on a canvas where the landscape was always going to be dark. If they had the wrong people guiding them, they often found themselves in dangerous situations where they had no understanding of the consequences, quickly lost control and made bad decisions. The seduction of immediate success through little effort poisoned good people, especially when the other roads to success looked impossible. Through seeing this, I developed the strength to withstand the enticement and seduction. I also saw, many times, the end result of taking the easy path in life, and it almost always set people back.

Through being competent at sport, there were choices available to progress through society. This is obviously a complimentary nod towards sport but also an indictment of the opportunities that were afforded to people of all colour and creeds at the lower end of the socioeconomic scale in Manchester in the early '90s. Joining a rock band or being an athlete were considered as equally credible options for employment as 'normal' jobs. A few of the local boys went to the local boxing club, which was attractive to me as I had the physique and speed to – in theory – excel at it. The sport of boxing has historically played a strong role for people of my social background, providing a release valve for in-built aggression and, for some, a way to escape the streets.

Sale West Amateur Boxing Club had a good name for its coaching and its embrace of local young athletes, but my first and only experience of boxing was not a good one. I realised that the discipline and control required to express your anger through boxing was foreign to my instincts. Allowing someone to thump your nose until it bleeds, while simultaneously controlling the rush of anger to the brain was something that would need more than one night of instruction for me. Athletics and boxing were very similar in that they created a controlled environment where you could visualise your anger and express it through your own actions. The only difference was that, with one of them, someone was punching and physically attacking you. I take my hat off to each and every person who enters the ring and has the ability to control those instincts. Boxers have the traits of warriors: they don't lack fear, but they can certainly smell it in others. This sense often comes from an innate understanding, bred on the street, of who is going to shirk and who is going to stand and fight.

One such person, from Sale West ABC, was Ricky Hatton. Ricky and I shared parallel career paths of sorts. He was from Stockport, a few miles away, but was also from a council estate background and had to literally fight his way up from the streets. We were, I believe, always vaguely aware that we were from the same area and, despite him being a few years younger, both conscious that our paths would have crossed many times during our childhood. Then again, there were as many mid-sized, white punchy characters from his area as there were sporty, mischievous black kids from mine. As our careers developed and coincided, he became a good friend. For him to rise to become a multiple world champion at multiple weights became an inspiration for me. He won his first world title by defeating Kostya Tszyu a few months after I won Olympic gold, which gave me immense pride. I had always wanted to prove that, even if you came from humble beginnings, there could be a path to greatness, and Ricky achieved the highest level of greatness his sport could bestow on him. At the time, as many boxing fans might recall, Tszyu was considered one of the best pound-for-pound boxers in the world and was a national hero in Australia. Ricky was given little or no chance of victory by even the most optimistic of boxing commentators. I have no doubt that Ricky's background contributed to him confronting, head-on, the immeasurable odds he faced in that contest, as we both had done in our personal lives from day one.

What Ricky and I shared was the notion of doing things the hard way. Neither of us were artificially engineered to perform, as many sports people these days are. It seems that instead of preparing the child for the journey they'll face, many coaches and parents nowadays believe it's their duty to smooth the road for the child instead. We weren't given a leg up by any academy or backer. In fact, at times it was quite the opposite, and it often felt as if there were hands on our shoulders holding us down. We were able to spot the sportsperson who'd been awarded scholarship, who'd had the professional coaching, and who had personal finance. For those people, doors were opened and progression enabled. In Ricky's case, he would always provide a wide council estate grin before battering them onto the canvas. For us, it wasn't about the social or financial gaps, merely, that in sports like boxing and athletics the result was more dependent on a primal action than a subjective skill. In golf, football, rugby, even maybe in swimming or cycling, a trained skill or understanding could overhaul any physical disadvantage a competitor had over you. Try that in a sport where you get beaten up, or find someone can simply run quicker than you. My career was winding down as Ricky's was on the up, but his demeanour, performances and drive gave me significant inspiration and impetus to carry on.

Another whose successful career could be traced back to his roots in Manchester council estates was the comedian and television personality Karl Pilkington. We were in school together, and his acerbic wit and stern-faced humour was evident even in those days. His tell-it-as-it-is cynicism that has so endeared him to millions, alongside Ricky Gervais and Stephen Merchant, was the default setting of many people who had grown up in our area and had seen the things we'd seen. He credits himself – wittily, and rightly so – with having a role in discovering my speed while we were playing go-karts together; a fact I will happily back up should he consider giving me an equal amount of credit for my role in his razor-sharp comedy. In truth, we did play a lot as children and he is probably right that he always wanted me to push him on the go-kart because I was the quickest and he would get the best start. I'm not sure if there is a linear progression from that to Olympic gold, but I'm sure that if there is he would be the one to find it.

While all this was going on, and as my burgeoning athletics career was developing well at Sale Harriers, I had discovered two things: firstly, that I had the beginnings of what might be called a sporting talent and, secondly, I now had the motivation to overcome the barriers that were blocking me. I learned, through my mother, the value of prioritising and focusing (the banning of sport to improve school grades taught me that), and in order to capitalise on the opportunity to make track and field a viable career option I had to squeeze every bit of talent from my body and mind – and that would take self-discipline.

Where would the discipline and good habits come from? Even I wasn't entirely sure. I had always wanted to impress others with physical feats, and finding the means to do just that in a structured and disciplined way ensured that I conformed with the norms expected of a track athlete. Also, my rebellious and argumentative nature subsided considerably as soon as I found myself on an athletics track with a coach. Despite it being a similar dynamic to school – where one figure of authority placed challenges on students to achieve – the situation at Sale Harriers, for me, was a million miles from Ashton-on-Mersey School. At the Harriers, despite my personal history being characterised by recklessness and a maverick bravado when being told what to do, I became very motivated and driven.

Sale Harriers athletics track is in the relatively leafy Wythenshawe district of Manchester, between Altrincham, Sale and Stockport. The green, red and white vest of the club has adorned the British athletics scene for many years and has a rich history of success, both as a club and with its athletes. Its remarkable achievements over many decades are due to its commitment to developing and engaging young athletes as well as providing the facilities to encourage and enthuse social athletes to take part and simply enjoy track and field. At the elite performance end of club, Sale Harriers has had a succession of strong teams competing in national leagues, proving that if you build a pyramid with a wider base the peak is often higher.

Mum had enrolled me as a Harrier when I was eight, and from the outset I enjoyed all aspects of being a track athlete, from the camaraderie forged in training, to the speed and strength gained from putting those hours in. It was also, for an eight-year-old, fun. It provided an outlet from a very early age and burned off the calories and the energy that might otherwise have been expended doing other more menacing and nefarious things. Athletics training not only made me energised and strong, it gave me focus and a purpose, with the added benefit of being too tired at the end of sessions to hang around street corners being a menace. By the age of 13, I was training with men which quickly hardened me as an athlete, as every training session was a level of competition I'd never previously experienced.

Sale Harriers made me feel really welcome. Because of the affluent nature of the surrounding areas – combined no doubt with the fact that you had to pay to use the track – the racial breakdown was primarily white working- to middle-class.. We all respected one another's abilities, sacrifices and efforts on the track; notions familiar to most club athletes. I felt that my running abilities were acknowledged and respected by club members – also, hopefully, my friendly and sunny disposition towards others – and that my skin colour was irrelevant. Yet this was not quite the case for all of them. I got on well with the parents of many of my fellow athletes right up until the moment I briefly started dating one of their daughters. Then, all of a sudden, to that father, the young talented sprinter became a black man. Despite hiding behind the social graces and overt politeness, skin colour was still an issue to many. Thankfully, that was to be an isolated incident at Sale Harriers, but such events are a constant reality for most black people in the UK, even three or four generations down the line.

Becoming a Sale Harrier didn't change my life, but it did show me that I needed to change my life. The Wythenshawe track was a safe place that I came to know. Prior to that, the concrete awfulness of the estate had been my entire world. The simple act of having to leave Sale Racecourse to be able to apply my talents in a slightly better part of Manchester became a metaphor that didn't take long for me to appreciate. That metaphor alone became an escape – a reason to get a little bit better at running, not for its own sake, but for the fact that it became a twice-weekly reason to venture outside of the circle. Sure, I was quick, and it didn't need a track and a pair of spikes to reveal itself as being self-evident, but deciding to become an Olympic champion merely in order to break out of Manchester wasn't a realistic life goal at that point, despite my lofty ambitions. The way I saw it, having that aspiration was no different or more likely to come to pass than the thousands of others who were brought up alongside me. They would have had the same aspirations of using Manchester United or Manchester City as their dream ticket to social mobility. It did show me, however, that there was life outside of what I had come to accept as my own world. It was also my pathway to achieve my dream, however unlikely, of emulating Carl Lewis and Jesse Owens.

As any track athlete will tell you, the training and preparation that goes on behind the scenes is a million miles away from the glamour of Olympic stadia and camera flashbulbs. It is especially so when you leave your home in a rough part of the North West of England and arrive at a wet track on blustery, damp, cold night to run on dimly-lit back straights until every sinew screamed with pain. It takes a certain form of masochism to endure taking your body to its limit, and then to do it again, before it's recovered. Dizziness, nausea, and a breathlessness that sucks your lungs dry is the reality of winter track training. The only satisfaction comes from looking at a clock, which is the sole judge of whether your performance was worthy of the effort. My memories of being a Sale Harrier include being a part of a wider family, with a camaraderie and sense of brotherhood, yet I can still recall standing on a white line, waiting for a coach to blow a whistle, while our breaths sent plumes of vapour into Manchester's cold night sky.

Pete Beavers, our coach, worked us hard, as did Tony, a local milkman who I used to work with, and finally Earl Tulloch, who was an international sprinter in his own right. Pete correlated hard work with progression and improvement, and although his was a philosophy I was to deviate from, at times, during my career, it was one which always proved correct. Often, as I lay on the side of the track, exhausted and cold, I questioned whether this truly was a release from life on the estate, or was I enjoying a surge of pain and angst by hurting myself through training? Either way, the satisfaction of training hard and the resultant improvements certainly made me feel better. The intervention of track and field at this time in my life in giving me such life lessons as discipline, focus and dedication proved absolutely critical. The reality is also stark: without this self-realisation I would have been destined to not only fail as a sprinter, but probably also in my quest to see the wider world outside of Manchester. Over thinking is often the curse of the runner, but as many who share my passion – whether through track running or jogging or endurance events – will testify, the thoughts that go through your head as you run often reveal your innermost guilt, pleasure and demons. Running 100 metres in training can last less than 11 seconds, but with the wrong thoughts filling your head it can feel like staring at the ceiling for hours, while questioning the point of your very existence.

This might explain my habit of taking my eye off the ball at times and I'm sure many of my peers at Sale Harriers got aggrieved by my rather horizontal nature around the track. Nothing in life to that point had been easy for me, or for my family, but what did come easily to me – relatively speaking – was this business of running quickly. I enjoyed the sensation of being good at something without having to invest as much effort or time into it as others. Many sprinters and middle distance runners at Sale Harriers would train, in the quest for personal improvement, until their bodies became sweating and vomiting machines. Despite the fact that I would endure my own fair share of this, there was no doubt that if and when the opportunity presented itself to operate at mid-range, I took it with both hands. Sprinters can absorb this attitude a little more than endurance athletes because our hundredths of a second improvements are often the result of more power and speed than the whole seconds of improvements at longer distances are created by blood, sweat and tears. However, had I been allowed to resort to my personal default setting – relaxed – too often, I would have certainly underachieved. These lessons were yet to be learned.

As the 1990s began I became better known in the local press for my athletics prowess, and also through national publications such as *Athletics Weekly*. My performances at age grade level were slowly translating into victories for Sale Harriers at more senior levels, and this made a few ears prick up. Selectors invited me to compete for regional events and, having won the 200m at the English Schools Championships, the path to higher levels of scrutiny and better competition came my way. I was now approaching the often travelled road of young athletes: would I be the 'next big thing' or the 'junior who failed to make the step up to senior'. To be honest, I found that challenge exhilarating. I enjoyed proving people wrong. The European Junior Championships, held at Thessaloniki, Greece, proved to be my own personal springboard. As a 17-year-old I won the 100m and 200m titles.

At that time, UK Athletics did not have a lottery funded programme (the National Lottery not being established until 1994) but, through small bursaries and by funding travel to training, they did provide support for athletes showing promise. A local businessman with whom I also trained with at Sale Harriers, Roger Kennedy, arranged a sponsored car for me, and a sum of money to enable me to stay away from the gangs, which was incredibly kind as I felt I had not truly earned that level of faith. Because of my advanced level of performances as a junior, I was training with the seniors at Sale and an unexpected consequence of this was that the adults at the club took me under their wing. Roger happened to be a part of our training group and I remain truly thankful for his thoughtfulness and generosity. The car was the coolest thing I had ever had. It was useful, naturally, getting to training – significantly easing the burden on my mum and Sophia – but it was also used for taking Lynx and the crew to Alton Towers. By this time Sophia was excelling academically and, due to her attending a private school, was socialising with children from a completely different socio-economic background in neighbouring Hale Barns. She would spend most of her time over at their plush houses but, strangely enough, none of her friends ever took the opportunity to come and play over at ours. Sophia was slowly but surely weaning herself off the effects of estate life.

A sporting discipline was forged on the track, but my natural instincts still came from the estate, where you could get hurt or even lose your life far too easily. Thanks to whatever physical talent I had, I could run from any danger; but nobody can outrun a bullet. As a teenager, going to parties, discos, house parties, and clubs were all part of the normal adolescent scene. However, where we would normally go, there were more gunshots than corks popping. Being in a nightclub or a party when someone brings out a gun is seriously scary and, despite the fact it shouldn't happen, it did on multiple occasions. Even to this day my instincts tell me, whenever I go into any building, to subconsciously be aware of where the emergency exit is. That instinct was forged growing up in Sale Racecourse.

The role models presented to us as young black men were completely alien to us and our circumstances. Trevor MacDonald presented *News at Ten* with intellectual aplomb and an articulation of speech that we had never experienced before. He didn't speak like anyone we knew, and his level of sophistication didn't resonate with a street guy from Manchester. As inspirational a figure as he was, he certainly wasn't anyone we could identify with. Purely from a diction standpoint, he spoke the Queen's English, not Queen Latifah's rap English that we preferred. Lenny Henry was another black man famous in Britain in the 1980s. Henry was pigeon-holed by the media into a niche so small that it undoubtedly suffocated his remarkable talent, and for him to portray black parodies on screen in his comedies, such as Theophilus Wildebeest, perpetuated the black stereotype. In order to find a spot on the airwaves he was reduced to portraying joke West Indians coming to Britain, listening to Bob Marley while talking Caribbean English. Whereas Henry might have been a role model, the characters he created certainly weren't.

We felt a need to connect with people in our own language, and via our own cultural preferences. We had to go overseas to find role models who had found success by being true to themselves, and who refused to fit into a particular cultural box. This is why Michael Jordan, Carl Lewis, and N.W.A. (Niggaz Wit Attitudes, the California-based hip hop group) became heroes for a whole generation of black British kids. In Jordan's case, his back story of being told in High School that he wasn't good enough, then becoming a world superstar, resonated far more than a newscaster with perfect diction.

This was 'reality' because Jordan's was a 'real' story. Fast forward 30 years, and the irony here is that there was more reality in Lenny Henry's characters than the so-called 'reality' television these days: a fact my children will have to process in order to find their own 'real life' role models. At least when we were kids we could recognise what was real and what was fake, unlike what is presented as reality on television and via the 'influencer' culture of today. Fakeness is now an industry and the end result is surely going to be frightening. My mum was worried because I was listening to gangster rappers from 6,000 miles away taking aim at each other on albums, whereas I am concerned about the mental health of our next generation who are struggling to decipher their reality – which is completely false and filtered – from within home-grown British popular culture.

My experience tells me that the impact this has, long term, is that many of the break-out heroes of inner-city life inadvertently end up hurting the societies where they came from. When a child ends up feeling significant pressure from peers, advertising, and idols to buy a particular boxer's merchandise, or wear the trainers a celebrity endorses, they put pressure on families to buy that stuff, when the truth is they can't afford it. Not wanting to let their child down they borrow, divert money from elsewhere, resort to the black market, or worse, to get what their child wants it, and then find themselves a target for others also want the same thing and are prepared to break the law to get it. This is the life experience of many in deprived communities since the advertising industry started targeting children, but it's getting worse. Children now spend hours on end on their phones, bombarded with imagery of 'street' clothes that cost hundreds of pounds, or headphones that cost six months' worth of pocket money. Even the icons being paid to act as influencers are getting manipulated. Our parents were not placed under such pressures to look or behave like stars. Parents will always feel inadequate under this incessant pressure unless they provide what their children crave.

Marva Campbell from Sale Racecourse estate in the late 1980s had enough worries on her plate in this regard. As much as my life on the track blossomed and changed, life on the streets stayed exactly the same. As was the norm with groups of young, aggressive boys, we were full of confidence and didn't care about anything or anyone. One of our mottos was, "Why do we need to sleep? We can sleep when we're dead". Unknown to us, a reality check was just around the corner.

A situation involving a friend of ours, 'T', had grown to the point where an argument had turned into aggression, and aggression into a longstanding feud, which inevitably escalated into hostility, with neither side's ego allowing them to back down. This tense situation only needed one spark to ignite real violence. Within our world, to that point, violence was measured on a scale from as painless as a punch or as painful as a blood wound. We were about to discover the true meaning of gang violence.

'T' was like a surrogate little brother to me and the rest of the crew. A constant theme of life on the streets was that small gangs always protected their younger members from the worst aspects of society. Mum was his Godmother, and our families were very friendly. I took every personal relationship seriously because the importance of being loyal and being tight to a crew was paramount, but the relationship we had through Mum always ensured that 'T' was given a little extra care and attention.

One of my friends received a call to say that there had been an incident, and that the police were already involved. This could either mean good news or bad news. Good news in respect that the consequence had already played out without us being there and, to be frank, we never entertained the thought of the bad news: "T has been shot."

There was no need to elaborate. The question, "But he is ok?" didn't follow. We knew from witnessing others having to deal with their own pain, that if someone was shot, there was a story and a circumstance to address immediately thereafter. We weren't given that luxury. We just had to process those fateful words.

Every ounce of energy in my body dropped to my toes like an icy deadweight. I was frozen to the spot. Time stood still. There was no difference between the sky and the horizon, and I couldn't hear a thing, just those fateful words on continuous repeat. This couldn't be happening. Lynx, 'T' and me had only recently spent some time together, laughing and joking about various silly things that young boys get up to. 'T' was not the kind of guy to let his mask down often and reveal his lighter side, and I had never seen him so engaging and happy with life as he was during what would be our final time together. He was a serious person who often felt more comfortable behind a shield of bravado, but there was no pretence and no ego involved in our interactions. He was just another lovely guy corrupted by the influences around us.

The emotion came flooding over me: "Who was it?" Then came anger, followed by rationalising: "What can I do?" Then anger and rage: "Where is he?" I was overwhelmed by a need to extract revenge, coupled with a sense that the world had halted on its axis. I felt sick and brave at the same time. Confusion. Screaming. Crying. Shivering.

I could have squeezed my fists hard enough to draw blood. Tears of ferocious rage filled my eyes.

We gathered together as a gang, our crew, and huddled in silence before the news broke far and wide and we were hurried back to our homes. I didn't sleep that night, and in all honesty I could not tell you how long it was before I had a good night's sleep. My face was blood-filled with rage and I felt as if I levitated above my bed that night as all my nerve endings tingled with the emotional energy coursing through my body.

Mike Tyson once said, "Everyone has a plan until they get punched in the mouth," and the truth was that we felt untouchable and immortal until tragedy came knocking at our door. Being hit with that body blow wasn't the worst feeling either – recovering from it was. We realised we could see the end game. As a consequence of one of our friends being murdered, we came to see reality in its full Technicolor horror. Seeing so much intense pain in his family's faces was a raw and harrowing feeling. Seeing a mother desperately trying to retain her dignity while contemplating the immensity of her loss was agonising. There was so much pain.

The days between the murder and the funeral were a living nightmare. We were all fragile and emotional, yet keen to project strength and vigour. The expected response was to talk about retribution, but against whom, and how? That response, though, was the antithesis of what was needed.

At the funeral, the open casket showed the true effects of this life of bravado and anger. That image became etched permanently on all of our minds. There was no need to say another word. As a member of a gang, whatever that had meant anyway, I was done. We had been through the anger. We had been through the feeling of wanting to instigate revenge. The end had come, and it was better for everyone if it ended now.

My mum went to the funeral. She never cried. She was far too formidable to display any emotion in public. This time, however, she cried. She cried for 'T' and his family's loss, but also in fear for what lay ahead for us if we weren't prepared to choose a different path. Mum had also heard whispers that members of our gang were potentially on a hit list.

One incident that brought this home was one Saturday, when Marlon and I were walking through the Royal Exchange shopping centre in Manchester. Mum had bought me a wonderful three-quarter length leather jacket, which I was proudly wearing while looking for clothes to enhance my wardrobe, when Marlon alerted me to the fact that five guys from a different crew were standing opposite us in the Exchange's courtyard. They had spotted us and were busy signalling to one another that we were there. Marlon knew that they were targeting him specifically so told me to leave as there would be less of a threat with just one person, and that this argument had nothing to do with me personally. I refused to leave, preferring to stand with a friend and take a beating out of loyalty: we were never going to win in a fight against five.

They came at us and we started fighting. We were surrounded and taking punches from all directions while trying to fight back until security guards or the police arrived, but no one came. The fight continued, five against two, and in the few seconds of respite where words were exchanged and blood wiped away before the next flurry of punches, we noticed the security guards gathered in a huddle simply watching it all unfold and instructing the public to walk away and continue with their shopping instead of gawping at a fully-fledged fight in the middle of the shopping centre.

It suddenly turned more hostile and very dangerous when one of the five revealed a knife and lunged at us both. I was lucky. The knife slashed through my coat, missed my midriff but left a six-inch gash in the leather. Heaven knows what damage that blade could have inflicted. The fight continued for around 15 minutes, to the point when they had had enough of beating us. We had managed to evade serious injury and left, albeit bloodstained, but with just a few bruises and sore heads. The realisation that trouble could find you from nowhere, even if you had done nothing to merit attracting it, was striking.

I decided to get the jacket patched up so Mum wouldn't notice the damage. Not only was I upset that my favourite item of clothing had been slashed, but concealing my troubles – and avoiding the inevitable motherly thunderstorm of disapproval that would have followed – was more important than almost being stabbed in the first place. Mum has been unaware of this episode, until now.

This was not the kind of life I wanted, but it was one that had been imposed upon me both circumstantially and geographically. The death of 'T' was a huge wake-up call and made a massive impact on me: "Can you leave Manchester now please Darren?" Mum pleaded.

I am proud of where I come from, because the world at Sale Racecourse wasn't always so bleak. It could be as dark or as bright as you wanted it to be, but mostly it was grey. It was that monotone greyness that motivated people to polarise and look for their own brightness or darkness. We certainly experienced the darkness. It was also hard to break out of such situations, and not just in a financial sense. It was sometimes easier to stay, especially with your extended family and friends also trapped by their circumstances. Everyone looked to others for leadership but I never wanted to be the leader. Anonymity was now impossible as I was becoming well known through athletics. This was when I decided to move.

3

Newport

"Everyone has a plan until they get punched in the mouth"
Mike Tyson

Manchester had claimed one victim, and I was wasn't planning on being another. 'T' was forever liberated from the threat of danger at every corner, and I was contemplating my next move. One which undoubtedly had personal safety in mind as much as professional progression.

The tragedy had ensured that every thought and every plan flew out of the window. All I had worked for, and achieved, suddenly felt insignificant and inconsequential. Every journey is a continuation from one destination to the next; yet every experience I had now felt as if it would have no bearing on what was to come next. There was a void. Bereavement and loss sucked the oxygen out of any decision-making capability I had. All I knew was that I was in danger of being consumed by my surroundings and that a fresh start would probably be a very good thing.

The kind of life that awaited me had I continued along the same path, was one which was now revealing itself to be the very one my teachers had predicted for a 'rough and ready' black kid with no academic interests. I had both the potential to be focused, yet was highly reckless when the red mist descended. Proof of my recklessness was when a Yamaha DT125 motorbike turned up on the streets one day, out of nowhere, and yours truly blazed around on it loudly and wildly until someone called the police and they chased me around the estate at high speed. None of us knew that it was a stolen bike, but the mentality in that place at that time – where attacks and stabbings were daily occurrences – was to give a mere shoulder shrug to such incidents of playful naughtiness. The bike was duly returned, with an apology and an acknowledgment of youthful idiocy, but to us, riding around on an abandoned bike was as natural as kicking a football if it had bounced out towards you on the street. The police, I am sure, saw it for the mindless japery that it was. To them, a loud noise and a small chase was small fry in a landscape where blood was regularly spilt.

There was also a huge fight in Blackpool, where the red mist had descended and I had lost control. A crew of ten of Lynx and Marlon's friends had gone go-karting in the town and stayed for a night out; chasing women, no doubt, but certainly not looking for any trouble. A few of the group were let in to the nightclub, and a few weren't. Things immediately got edgy with the bouncers, and once – in their own inimitable way – they laid their hands on us, the retaliatory fists came flying. Ten people fighting ten became a 30-strong melee once reinforcements arrived from a neighbouring pub's security team, and before we knew it a large number of policemen had arrived at the scene. A member of security had pushed me around and I completely lost control of my senses. It turned nasty very quickly. Considering our backgrounds, and what we experienced every day, if people were willing to push us to 'that place', where violence reigned and niceties abandoned, there would be no rules and no limits shown from us either.

Marlon had articulated this weakness in our nature while on a trip to Bilbao. He often said that when living a life on the streets, where some people are protected whatever they do, fear abandons you as a defence mechanism. The feeling of being able to do what you want, when you want, is not only reinforced daily but becomes a part of your personality. I knew where to draw the line as far as showing people the same respect as they showed me, but I always knew that I had the capability to rely on aggression and power if it became necessary in any stand-off situation. Having similar people of a similar vein around multiplied that feeling.

The trip to Bilbao was a laughable farce, something out of a Monty Python sketch. Lynx, Marlon and a few of the crew had heard of a cheap boat trip to the Basque city that allowed for some shopping, sightseeing and fun before returning a few days later. The journey itself was half the attraction – over a day on a luxury ferry with a bar and entertainment with nothing but the sea for company. We were all well up for it and turned up, not exactly expecting a cruise liner but at least a decent and comfortable ship for the journey. What we were presented with was a rickety old banger which would have surely sunk if it had collided with a seagull. Within minutes of departing the harbour on this swaying steel raft, seasickness kicked in and it quickly became vomit-central – all except for Lynx who had acquired sea legs from somewhere and was busy laughing himself through the whole experience. I threw up non-stop for hours on end, the kind of relentless vomiting which didn't get better even after I had nothing left to throw-up.

Bilbao was a washout. We sat in the sun, hands on heads, awaiting our return journey on the dinghy of death. Once we returned to – I believe it was Plymouth but it felt like the depths of a haunting underworld – we were in foul, aggressive, gang mode. We had vomited ourselves empty, had suffered headaches for hours, and were contemplating a six-hour drive back to Manchester all crammed into one car. We strolled through immigration – a group of nasty angry looking black guys with no luggage to speak of but faces carved with anger – and were hastily approached by the gentlemen in Customs and Excise. I angrily pointed to one of them and, with a tone borne of pure fatigued hostility, said: "Don't even fucking think about pulling us over now mate," and stared at him with my eyes red with furious indignation. To my surprise (now – not then) he backed away and his colleagues did the same. No rational, reasonable person raised in a normal upbringing would have dared, or even considered acting in such a way to a servant of Her Majesty's Government. To think that it even happened is incredible, but estate people in Manchester weren't normal people and often, sadly, we didn't think the rules of society applied to us. It was because of that attitude and the trouble it created for me I had to reconsider my path.

Lynx and I – trusted lifelong friends – considered our futures. I also had to bring my mum's wellbeing into the equation. Previously I had *suspected* that she had fears about something terrible happening to her son on the estate, whereas now I *knew* she was thinking this. Once the emotion from the funeral subsided, some clarity appeared. Yet I could not get the images of the body and my mum's weeping face out of my mind. We had spoken during that time of heightened emotion about moving away, and despite the emotional wounds being horrifyingly raw, this still seemed a sensible option as logic and composure slowly returned. We had family in London, where I could combine a new start with joining a strong training group. Bruce Longden, Sally Gunnell's coach, lived in London and Malcolm Arnold, Colin Jackson's coach lived in Wales. These were my two options. I was keen to stay away from London because there would have been bad influences there that could have dragged me back to the dark side (so to speak).

I was at an important junction on my life journey. One turn would probably lead to more darkness and pain, whereas the other offered the strong possibility of light and opportunity. Being a young black man in Manchester there was the ever-present issue of guilt through association. People around me were forever suspected of various things whether through crime or mischief, and one small incident always had the potential to grow and cause wider problems. I remember one specific occurrence when I had been fortunate enough to be invited to a training camp in Australia with athletes who were at the top of the sport – Colin Jackson and Linford Christie among them.

Before flying out, and along with two friends who were in my car at the time, I was arrested by the police because sometime during the previous week I had been in the company of someone they wanted to speak to. I was taken to the police station and held for questioning, even taking part in an ID parade (as one of the innocent third parties, I hasten to add). We were held overnight and, when we woke up, realised that three more of our friends had also been detained. When following up on their investigation it became apparent that I was heavily tainted by association.

This was problematic and had the potential to multiply exponentially for me, for I would not have been able to leave the country and fly to Australia if charged with anything. This was the reality for black men living where we were and, if anything, it solidified my rationale for moving away. Manchester wasn't like London as far as street life was concerned: everything in my world fell within a radius of five miles, where everyone knew everyone else. You were always one person's testimony away from being called in for questioning. I didn't want the spectre of a police cell depriving me of what I thought were my life's opportunities. I wanted to bring pride to the family, not shame, but thankfully the incident was resolved and I was off to Australia.

The curveball route leading to south Wales was strengthened further in Australia due to the personal traits I saw in one man: Colin Jackson. I had never seen anyone with as much drive and determination to succeed. His preparation, his detail, his depth of knowledge in his event, and his quest for perfection was staggering. Here was an athlete already with an Olympic medal in his pocket, yet still forensic in his approach to self-improvement. He knew every second, every inch, every weight, and every aspect of his training. I had come from the streets, where a relaxed and laid back approach to day-to-day life was the norm. Colin's style was to spend hours seeking perfection, even through the perpetual analysis of his own performances was obsessive. However, in time, I came to understand that he was operating at the highest level of performance. I liked what I saw and I could see how being around someone like Colin could have a huge influence on my own approach.

Many athletes had talked about the superb range of facilities in Wales. There were fully synthetic athletic tracks in Cwmbrân, Newport and Cardiff – all within ten miles of one another. There was also the famous (or infamous) Merthyr Mawr sand dunes a few junctions down the M4 – a place synonymous with Steve Ovett – where world-class athletes worked on their strength and endurance during the off-season. More importantly, there was a small cohort of genuinely world-class athletes there (Colin, Paul Gray and Jamie Baulch among others). Spending time competing with and against such individuals ensured that everyone knew what the other was up to domestically, and all the vibes coming back from Wales were good. It sounded like a good place to train without the distractions of big city life, and a place where, as an athlete, a strong work ethic could co-exist with rest and relaxation. In the context of what I had been experiencing, it became the preferred option, since it sounded completely the opposite of what I was used to. In direct contrast to the step that most late-teenagers take, I decided to move away from the big city lights of Manchester to a more sedate and slower paced life in the south Wales valleys. I was lucky enough to occasionally stay with 400m runner Adrian Patrick's parents in Slough, and with my second cousins Mark, Andrew and

Andrea Walcott in Wolverhampton. However, once the decision to relocate was made, there was some time to go before I made the move and I had the World Junior Championships to contend with first.

There was no doubt that during this period my day-to-day life was getting worse, but my athletics was getting better, and the opportunities athletics offered me were increasing also. In early August 1992, a letter arrived at Edgbaston House, Birmingham, from the USA. The letter had come from the University of Notre Dame in Indiana, a state located just below Lake Michigan and above Kentucky, the birthplace of the 'Louisville Lip' himself, Muhammad Ali. Many consider this area of the USA to be the epicentre of world sport. Surrounding the Great Lakes in the American Midwest are the Green Bay Packers, the Chicago Bulls, the Indianapolis Colts, the Chicago White Sox and the Detroit Red Wings. Muhammad Ali, Michael Jordan, Sugar Ray Robinson and Magic Johnson all, at some point, called the Midwest 'home'.

The cherry on the cake, however, is that located in South Bend, Indiana, is the University of Notre Dame, a name synonymous with American football. This is one of the cathedrals of American sport, and the home of one of the strongest collegiate sports traditions worldwide. The legendary San Francisco quarterback Joe Montana played here, and over 500 NFL players have passed through the gates of Notre Dame Stadium as students, wearing the famous 'Fighting Irish' navy and gold strip. During the 2020 NFL season alone, an incredible 44 NFL players were former players of the University of Notre Dame, enough for four on-field teams. Meanwhile, 150 miles up the road – which in American terms is a hop, skip and a jump – in Ann Arbor, my childhood idol Jesse Owens had performed what *Sports Illustrated Magazine* had described as being the 'greatest 45 minutes ever in sport'. At the 1935 Big Ten collegiate championships, Ohio State University's Owens broke four track and field world records in three-quarters-of-an-hour: a feat that's scarcely believable. The history and legacy of this area is almost unparalleled.

The letter had come to the British Athletics Federation (now UK Athletics) and marked for my attention. It was from the University of Notre Dame's assistant track coach, and was inviting me to express an interest in becoming a 'student-athlete' with them. I had never considered life as a student, and the only degree I would have been a Masters in Ignorance of what it took to enter higher education. I remember dismissing it as soon as I had read it. Gaining notoriety for being a rising star in track and field led to many things, I figured, and this was merely one of them. I was not going to run away from everything and everyone I knew when things were going so well; and from an athletic perspective they were about to get a lot better for me, despite my own efforts.

The 1992 World Junior Athletics Championships held in Seoul, South Korea, became a springboard for many athletes. A young athlete named Haile Gebrselassie won the 5,000m and 10,000m double (with Hicham el Guerrouj taking bronze behind him in the shorter distance), and soon-to-be world superstar Cathy Freeman took a step closer to being a household name in Australia by taking the silver medal in the 200m. The highly respected administrator and coach Frank Dick, who had a guiding hand in the direction of UK Athletics at the time, had the forethought of using these championships as a test run for the 1996 Olympics. He wanted the British junior athletes to form the nucleus of a team to launch an assault on Atlanta four years later. Admittedly, I had undertrained all winter – falling under the often-travelled curse of believing talent would take me through. As a result, that summer underperformed badly leading up to the Games, and was only getting close to being fit enough to compete by actually racing. By the time I arrived in Seoul I was in the kind of shape I should have been for the first race of the season, as opposed to peaking and achieving new standards in a world competition. Fortunately, I was running senior times as a junior and this gave me the confidence to overachieve when 'stepping down' an age group, so to speak.

Yet, as any athlete will tell you, having the ability to run a race fast once is simply the first step. Each event has up to four races to merely reach the final; therefore having an ability to recover quickly and re-perform at the highest level forms the basis of any good athlete. That ability itself is dependent on a strong tough winter training block. This I hadn't done. Despite, finally, running some quick times leading up to South Korea, the combination of my poor conditioning level and the workload of heats, semis and finals in Seoul (as well as running the 100m, 200m and relays) left me absolutely exhausted. I finished second to Ato Boldon of Trinidad in both sprint events but, along with Allyn Condon, Jason Fergus and my good friend Jamie Baulch, won gold in the relay and broke the junior world record. However, despite this success and the plaudits generated, the correlation between not putting in the hard work and the resultant underperformances at my own individual events stayed with me for life.

Having won three medals in Seoul, two silvers and a gold, compared to the UK team winning a total of four medals (Steve Smith, the high jumper, was the other medallist, securing gold), my profile was raised considerably back home. Being only 19, I was not a familiar name to viewers of British athletics, so any hyperbole about a new talent bursting on to the scene could have done more harm than good. A slow, purposeful climb to the top of sport is always the best path since you learn lessons and failures along the way. 'Exploding' on the scene can cause problems where an athlete can start believing the hype.

I should have felt immense personal satisfaction at my achievement. The truth was, however, that after my relay performance I went behind the stand and cried tears of frustration. The Olympic Stadium in Seoul – forever etched in the memory of sport as the scene of the most infamous race in history where Ben Johnson won the Men's Olympic 100m in 1988 and then got disqualified – became a symbol of reaping what I had sown. I promised myself, there and then, that I would lose the nonchalant and relaxed attitude I had, and that I would, at the very least, always look to be the most fierce competitor I could possibly be.

A few weeks after returning home another letter arrived from the University of Notre Dame. It was almost a carbon copy of the first, but this time it also complimented me on my performances at the World Juniors. It wouldn't have mattered had they sent four more. I had already dismissed anything that would have interrupted me staying with my friends and preparing to be an Olympic athlete. My mother saw the opportunity, recognised its significance, and tried to convince me to put time aside to consider its merits. I was reminded by Sophia that Mum's last words to her on her first day at 'prep' school was that she was there for education, and nothing else. The importance of learning was not lost on the Campbell girls. I, however, was immature, and ignorant. I should have listened to Mum, but I didn't. I was also badly misadvised. In the '90s, offers for sports scholarships to foreign students from such prestigious universities in the United States of America were very rare. Being asked twice was a huge compliment. The narrative in the UK, however, was that the American collegiate circuit (known as the National Collegiate Athletic Association - NCAA) was a one-way road to burn out. Many coaches told me that the American system would run me ragged: "They will absolutely break you," said others. The truth was they might have been right, but their advice was dominated by the narrow lens of track and field athletics, with little or no consideration for my personal development.

The people advising me were completely misreading the context. A young black man from Sale Racecourse happened to be a quick runner, and was offered the opportunity for a full scholarship at a world-renowned sporting institution, where education, life experience and an exceptionally high level of athletic competition would have been provided for him. This simply didn't happen to kids from our estate. What could have been a phenomenal, life-altering experience, was swatted away through unfamiliarity, and maybe a little fear of the unknown. Also, the NCAA system regularly created Olympic champions: Jesse Owens, studied at Ohio State University, while Carl Lewis went to the University of Houston. Ato Boldon must have received a similar letter upon his return from Seoul because he enrolled at the University of California Los Angeles (UCLA) and became NCAA champion in 1996. The general narrative at the time was that I was progressing nicely in track and field and why let an uncontrollable variable interrupt that growth. The problem was, it was uncontrollable for them and not for me.

It was such decisions that would ultimately lead me to learn the value of appreciating each opportunity, as it presented itself, especially as a parent. Mum had made the conscious decision to support us in each and every way possible within her limited means and time available, which meant that my sister Sophia pursued academia and it was athletics for me. This wasn't a tunnel-vision approach however, jettisoning all other opportunities at the expense of one goal. This may explain why Mum's was the only voice at the time advocating considering going to America to study.

Sophia went on to become a news editor at a radio station, and then a primary school teacher, an occupation she cherishes despite the challenges it produces. The injustice in this situation was that it should have been budding teachers and useful contributors to society like Sophia who should have been the recipients of offers to study and expand their experiences around the world, not their brothers who happened to be able to run quickly in a straight line. True, we had been lucky as a family to pass all the means-tested thresholds to merit Sophia getting an 'assisted place' at a school where her fees, travel and uniform were paid for, but I was handed a winning lottery ticket with a potential scholarship to Notre Dame and I had no comprehension of what I was missing out on.

Looking back, through the lens of what has ultimately been a successful career, there are no regrets on my decision not to go, but the fact that officials from UK Athletics heavily dissuaded me from going at the time makes me think that I may have been viewed as an athletic asset to them as opposed to them caring for my future well-being. There is no doubt I would have received a wonderful education and life experience in the US. However, this was the time before the internet, there was little real-world advice available, and nobody that we knew of at the time had gone through the experience themselves and could give guidance. Years later, when I was invited to join the team at BBC Sport, I could call upon Ian Wright as a sounding board to give his advice and share his experiences, which was priceless, but in that situation, in those circumstances and at that time it was a leap in the unknown for me. Only now do I realise how much of a huge deal and an enormous honour it was to have been offered that potentially life-changing opportunity.

The Seoul World Junior Championships taught me the valuable lesson that the essentials for success weren't just limited to just running quickly. At major championships, all sprinters need the fitness to be able to repeat their performances over four rounds in two to three days – bearing in mind also that most sprinters think they can double up on the 100m and 200m while also being called up for the 4 x 100m relay. What was also crucial was having the experience of being able to do all this naturally, under pressure, where you get only one chance to get it right.

So, how could I replicate this? Strictly speaking I couldn't, but I decided to adopt the lessons of Seoul the best I could. For example, in order to be in peak condition, physically and mentally, I would always run in the British Athletics League – the domestic team-based competition in the United Kingdom – that mainly featured club and social athletes. The elite runners, despite technically being members of these clubs, would mostly stay away from this level of competition. I competed solely because I needed races. I needed to iron out my performances, to shake off the cobwebs so to speak, from winter training. I wanted those little mistakes that appear in competitive sprinting (such as false starts, slow starts, rusty techniques) to reveal themselves in races where the time didn't matter and where I finished in the race wasn't important. I purposefully placed myself under the pressure of the race environment early in the season, to tease out these errors.

Training and racing is different – like a boxer would compare sparring and fighting. I would see a crucial part of my preparation for big races as getting the errors out in the smaller races without the scrutiny of times, standards and medals. I would often, even as a junior, get double-take glances from fellow competitors at Cobham, Barnet Copthall or Leckwith, in disbelief that I would be there representing Sale Harriers and, as a result, I would often get more nervous running in the British League than at the Olympics. Racing at this level, therefore, gave me the race experience, the exposure to mistakes, and competitive anxiety: all immeasurable aspects of my preperation.

Since the advent of the Santa Monica Track Club in the early 1980s with its superstar members such as Carl Lewis, Joe DeLoach, Leroy Burrell (and Carl Lewis' sister Carol, herself a long jump bronze medalist at the 1983 World Championship), there had been a noticeable increase in the concept of 'massed talent' training within track and field. The emergence of the Rift Valley Kenyan runners who dominated middle distance running provided another example. During the late 1980s, the likes of Colin Jackson, Linford Christie and Mark McCoy (all world champions and record holders) trained together. Track and field athletics is essentially an individual sport; however, there is often a collective understanding that in order to perform with the best you have to train with the best. Many of the world's best train with each other in order to maintain high standards of performance while also potentially condensing the talent pool in order to distance themselves from the rest of the competition. An inadvertent by-product of this concept is also the minimalisation of mediocrity, with all its associated benefits.

Following many heart-to-heart conversations with Mum and Sophia about the way forward for me in athletics, and in life, I finally made the decision to move to Wales. One of UK Athletics', indeed, World Athletics' finest coaches, Malcolm Arnold, lived in south Wales and he ran a small coaching group based around the Newport and Cardiff area. His coaching successes included the 1972 Munich Olympics 400m hurdles champion John Akii-Bua, future Olympic 110m hurdles champion Mark McCoy, world champion and world record holder Colin Jackson, as well as other phenomenal athletes such as Nigel Walker, Paul Gray and Kay Morley.

Moving from Sale Racecourse to Aberbargoed was like moving to another world, and Malcolm was kind enough to invite me to his home for a brief period while I organised my living arrangements. This had been coal mining country for over 100 years, and its decline during the Thatcher years had mirrored the lack of investment and care synonymous with Moss Side. Where previously there had been thriving communities based around the mines, chapels and rugby fields, there were now villages that no longer had any functional or geographical reasons for existing other than to provide commuter belt houses for those working in Cardiff. Up the road, in neighbouring Pontllanffraith, at the same time I moved to Wales in the early 1990s emerged the Manic Street Preachers, whose songs and message revolved around proud and educated communities left behind by rampant capitalism. We were both based in the heart of the former coalmining valleys of Wales and, in our own ways, preparing to take on the world's greatest stadiums.

I was fortunate enough to be able to line up against the likes of Colin, Nigel Walker and Paul Gray on a daily basis – exceptionally quick athletes who would always look to raise the bar. Nigel, having not qualified for the 1992 Barcelona Olympics, was to eventually leave athletics to play rugby union for Cardiff and Wales with great success, before becoming Head of Sport at BBC Wales. Consequently I didn't get to spend too much time with him in an athletics capacity. He went on to score 12 tries in 17 Test matches, a phenomenal strike rate in international rugby. These were athletes either at the top of their game or had been there and done it. Amassing a small but determined group of people with high standards enabled all members of our training group to push each other and demand more from one another. When we trained we represented ourselves within an elite training group yet, when we competed, we represented the training group while also seeking pride and glory for ourselves as individuals. It would be a stretch, maybe, to suggest that Malcolm's training group in Wales at that time was the British equivalent of the Santa Monica Track Club but, in retrospect, with the amount of gold medals and Olympic success that group achieved, we weren't that far off. The standards and expectation of performance from Malcolm was high, and he tolerated no mediocrity whatsoever.

I was fortunate enough, as a 19-year-old, to go to the 1993 World Athletics Championships in Stuttgart, Germany. I had been selected as a part of the 4 x 100m relay squad having finished fifth in the UK National Championships 100m that year but, in reality, I was going for the experience. The attitude of the UK coaching structure at the time was not only to oversee high performance but also to cultivate experiences for the future. I was a teenage pain in the backside whose attitude, even on the flight over, was to question every single reason for my presence there, since it was relatively obvious that I would not play any significant part in the relays themselves. I am sure that for many of the senior athletes, who were in many cases looking for that peak moment in their careers, I was a nightmare, with my presence probably being a distraction at best. Yet, as an exercise in educating the potential stars of tomorrow, from UK Athletics' standpoint, it was a master-stroke. I spent time with gold medal winners from all countries – watching them warm up, interact, and behave off-track. My childhood idol Carl Lewis was there, and rubbing shoulders with him as a competitor, not as a fan, was surreal.

I found the experience of watching others warm up and prepare boring and unfulfilling, up until the point that Linford snapped and angrily urged me to recognise what I could learn from the other athletes. It was more of a thrill for me to help Linford choose the interior of the Mercedes he would win by winning gold than learning from those around me. One of the more revealing insights of this peek-behind-the-curtains experience was in the pre-race build up. Seeing world stars such as Linford Christie, Michael Johnson, Sergey Bubka and Jan Železný in the warm-up areas under the stand, struggling to control their nerves and looking incredibly vulnerable and edgy, was an eye-opener to say the least. In Linford's case especially, I thought he was a hard man from the street and one of life's tough guys, but even he looked unsettled and anxious prowling around the stadium's tunnels before the event. How he would metamorphosize on track into an unbeatable colossus of alpha male assurance taught me that many were adopting a persona and creating an aura of strength as a façade. Linford taught me that you can beat someone before you race them, and that you can even beat someone's confidence up without beating them up. There was no doubt that Linford's aura immediately before races intimidated some of his competitors.

From the British team's perspective, this was a genuine golden era. Linford won gold in the men's 100m (which I saw from the amazing vantage point of the tunnel at the end of the track). Colin Jackson won a superb 110m hurdles gold, breaking the world record in the process, and providing one of the most amazingly dramatic finishing photographs in any athlete's career, with a violent finger-pointed punch as he crossed the line indicating his relish at achieving his dream. Tony Jarrett, his friend, came second in a British one-two. John Regis took 200m silver, while Mick Hill and Steve Smith took bronze in the javelin and high jump respectively. The wonderful Sally Gunnell won gold in the 400m hurdles to add to her Olympic title in Barcelona the previous year, and 'my' squad, the men's 4 x 100m relay took silver. It was British Athletics riding the crest of a very high wave indeed, and it was exhilarating as a young athlete to be able to experience it. On the flight home, my thoughts were how the Games had given me experience, inspiration, enjoyment and life lessons. That was quite a change from what I was expecting on the flight out.

4

Wilderness

"The day you feel that you have to take drugs to be the best, stop —
because it's not that serious."
Marva Campbell

Having had first-hand experience of witnessing the effect drugs had
on an individual, and on the severe repercussions a drug culture has
on society, my personal opinion concerning drugs in sport was not
forged on any theoretical or moral platform, but from an instinctive
reaction based on personal understanding. We had to dodge needles
on the playground as kids, and we had to clear needles from the grass
of the football field as teenagers. Drugs were a part of society we
always knew to stay away from.

As holier-than-thou and sanctimonious as it may sound to hold a
values-based opposition to drugs in sport, that wasn't necessarily just
my stance. I simply saw that wherever a drug problem existed, whether
in society or in sport, it had its own gravitational pull on poverty;
poverty of behaviour, poverty of action and poverty of finance.
Because of my background, I also equated illegality with the notion
of trust. If you decided to take drugs from someone, you were totally
reliant on that individual providing exactly what had been offered.
You were also reliant on that person not coming back to demand a
price for their silence. These were the realities of life for those involved
with drugs, both on the street and in sport.

Drugs were all around us growing up on the Sale Racecourse estate, and seeing a person fall into a dark hole because of their effects was commonplace. I must have seen it 10 or 15 times while I was growing up. It shaped my view of most illegal drugs and on the environment within which they fester. Seeing a beautiful person, girl or boy, get swallowed up by crack cocaine or heroin is pitiful, like the gradual wilting of a human flower. You see each petal fall off and left discarded one by one, until all you see is a stalk devoid of nutrients and life. I vividly remember one case involving a pretty young girl who was a few years younger than me, but whose experience I shared trying to carve out an existence on the streets of Manchester. I will call her 'Poppy'.

At the time she was of late high school age, and was known for her bubbly personality, her beauty, and her sunny disposition. She was the kind of person you would want to be around. As kids on the estate, we knew each other, so to see her demise from afar was heart-breaking, knowing that none of us could have any influence over her fall. Her beauty was the ultimate commodity in a world where you had to fight for everything you had. The cars, the money, the clothes – these things had to be earned and worked for, even when the means of earning them was dishonest – and yet she had been given something that society accepted as important: astounding beauty. With those who 'ran the streets,' there was a measure of equity between having the materialistic goods, and the association with beauty. They wanted her around them because she was pretty and that was a status symbol for them.

In a classic case of Stockholm Syndrome, Poppy also wanted to be around those self-proclaimed 'successful' people with the big expensive cars and the money. In that environment it would reflect well on her as well as on those she wanted to impress. There were also those who just loved to see people with more than them suffer, or fall from grace. Eventually she became the flower that grew too tall and needed to be pruned.

One way of ensuring someone suffered and struggled was through the introduction of drugs. Some of the drugs available at the time were of the worst kind. Heroin takes no prisoners. Soon enough, chasing what she thought would make her happy broke her. She was corrupted by those who pretended to care for her, through introducing her to a world from which attempts to escape were doomed. The physical

The young Darren Andrew Grant.

With my mum (Marva) and baby sister (Sophia).

Celebrating my sister's birthday.

Growing up fast at Sale Racecourse.

At Princess Road Primary School, Moss Side (I'm top right).

Taking centre stage at Ashton-on-Mersey secondary school, Sale.

Marlon (left) and Tommy (centre) were my mates at school and we've remained good friends ever since.

Darren's dash

TRAFFORD Schools turned on the style with a series of medal-winning performances in the Greater Manchester Schools Athletics Championships at Longford Park.

The winners are hoping for selection to the county team for the English Schools Championships at Derby on July 13 and 14, but victory at the county championships is not enough to guarantee selection as the county usually requires their competitors to have achieved the national qualifying standard.

Certain to be at Derby is Ashton-on-Mersey sprint ace Darren Campbell (pictured above) who equalled the championship best mark in the intermediate 200 metres with a time of 22.3.

The Mersey flier already holds the junior record with his time of 23.3 last year and he made it a double despite appalling weather conditions and carrying a slight injury.

By the late 1980s my performances were getting noticed.

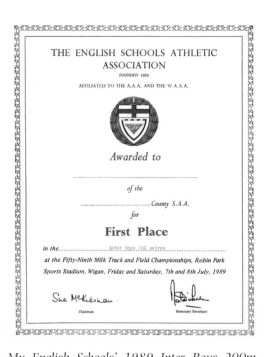

THE ENGLISH SCHOOLS ATHLETIC ASSOCIATION

FOUNDED 1925

AFFILIATED TO THE A.A.A. AND THE W.A.A.A.

Awarded to

of the

County S.A.A.

for

First Place

in the..............Inter Boys 200 metres..............

at the Fifty-Ninth Milk Track and Field Championships, Robin Park Sports Stadium, Wigan, Friday and Saturday, 7th and 8th July, 1989

Sue McKiernan.
Chairman

Honorary Secretary

My English Schools' 1989 Inter Boys 200m winner's certificate. They didn't bother to insert my name.

Representing Trafford Schools at the English Schools Championships.

Anchoring the 4 x 100m for Trafford Schools

It was a huge thrill to be interviewed by the inspirational Helen Rollason.

1989 British Rail Sprinter Youth 100m champion, with my 'arch rival' David Jackson (right).

Darren sprints to personal record

MANCHESTER METRO NEWS 18.8.89

SALE sprinter Darren Campbell stormed to an impressive victory and a new personal record at the Kodak AAA Championships in Birmingham on Saturday.

Campbell's time of 10.80 seconds was enough to win him the British Rail Sprinter Trophy Youths Final, beating his arch rival David Jackson of Wombwell.

Jackson, previously unbeaten at the distance this season, led for the first 60 metres of the race eventually being beaten into second.

Athletics

The Sprinter Trophy Series continues at the Kodak Classic in Gateshead with the senior men's and women's finals.

Darren Campbell

My victory and personal record made the news.

Proudly showing off my winner's trophy at the AAA Championships in Birmingham.

Representing Sale Harriers.

A winner with my six-a-side football team.

Beating Mark Walcott to win the 100m national youth title.

Dipping in front of David Jackson to win at the Birmingham Alexander Stadium

Fellow Sale Harrier and local businessman, Roger Kennedy, generously arranged my first sponsored car.

I was so honoured to receive offers of a scholarship to the prestigious University of Notre Dame in the United States ...

... and another from the University of Idaho. My mum told me to go – they were amazing opportunities – but I took the advice of others and decided against. It's too late to wonder 'What if?', but I'll always remain grateful for the invitations.

My growing success led to a car upgrade to this beautiful Jaguar.

Darren Campbell, semi-professional footballer, with Weymouth FC (back row, second from left).

I really enjoyed my 27 games with Weymouth FC, 'the Terras', which included a goal against a Canadian team in a pre-season friendly - my only 'international' goal. My strength and speed were great assets as I strove for success on the south coast. (Photos © idrismartin@wordpress.com)

Scoring one of my four goals for Weymouth.

PLYMOUTH ARGYLE FOOTBALL CO LTD

HOME PARK · PLYMOUTH PL2 3DQ

Telephone: Company Office - (0752) 562561 Commercial Department - (0752) 569597
Far Post Club - (0752) 556701 Football & Community Development - (0752) 606710
Lottery Department - (0752) 561041 Shop - (0752) 558292
Facsimile: (0752) 606167

Founded in 1886

Your Ref:

Our Ref:

without Prejudice

Basic wage £250 p/week = £13,000

Appearance money when playing in recognised 1st Team matches £100 p/game (46 × 100) = £4,600

Board & Lodging (£55 × 52) = £2,860

Additional bonus after 25 recognised 1st team games = £5,000

Additional bonus after 40 recognised first team league/cup goals. = £5,000.

The offer from Plymouth Argyle came in after I'd committed to Weymouth, but the handwritten contract shows the financial realities of lower league football.

My return to athletics saw me reunited with training partners and good friends, Jamie Baulch and Paul Gray.

Competing in a race, with Linford Christie, during a training camp in Australia.

1998 proved to be a huge year for me, and justified my return to athletics. First up was victory in the 100m at the AAA Championships, ahead of Dwain Chambers and Jason Gardener.

Then came success with Team GB, at the 1998 Europa Cup.

What a feeling! Winning the gold medal and becoming the European 100m champion in Budapest.

The celebratory embrace with my inspirational coach Linford Christie says it all.

European gold tasted so good.

DARREN CAMPBELL revealed yesterday how his European gold medal will take him back to Moss Side to tell the youths on the streets how sport can help them find a better way of life.

The new champion was all smiles on the morning after his 100 metres victory and still coming to terms with how his achievement in the Nep Stadium will affect his lifestyle.

Watched by a beaming Linford Christie, his coach and mentor, and with Grand Prix organisers already offering him races all over the world, Campbell recalled his days growing up among the terraced streets of Manchester.

FORMER Cwmbran Town player Darren Campbell is the European 100m champion – and he still misses his football.

Campbell was the original 'new Linford' and was even tipped by Britain's greatest athlete as his natural successor six years ago,

But Campbell became disillusioned with athletics and – being Manchester-born and bred – it was only natural he would turn to football.

He played with Plymouth Argyle in the football league and then had a spell with non-league Weymouth Town before moving to play for Tony Willcox's Cwmbran in the League of Wales.

"Darren was a popular lad with the players and he still comes and watches us from time to time," said Willcox.

How my triumph was reported: The Independent (above, left) and Newport's South Wales Argus (above, right). Very different takes, but I loved them both.

Celebrating my gold medal at the Szechenyi Thermal Baths, Budapest.

Another victory, and another European gold medal, in the 4 x 100m, with (L-R) Allyn Condon, Julian Golding, and Dougie Walker.

Welshman Iwan Thomas also became European champion in Budapest, in the 400m.

My golden year ended with victory in Kuala Lumpur for England at the Commonwealth Games 4 x 100m with (L-R), Julian Golding, Marlon Devonish and Dwain Chambers.

Putting on the style, with Paul Gray.

Enjoying the company of good friends (L-R), Andrew Walcott, Paul Gray, Bruny Surin, Adrian Patrick and Linford Christie.

and mental scars of drug use did not take long to take hold. We saw from afar as her eyes become cold, her skin pale and blotchy, and her interactions with others became steely and sharp-tongued. Gone was the happy-go-lucky girl.

Everyone, everywhere was a threat. Then her life force disappeared. Her hoodie became a permanent fixture, covering her head and hiding her once-beautiful face from the world, and her desperation could only be measured in respect of her changing from 'one of us' to being 'one of those'. For Poppy, as with countless others, drugs became a form of escapism, and once she was on that journey, and realised – in her sober moments – how far she had plunged, she needed to decide what she really wanted. More escapism, of course, was her answer, and that came through more drugs. The speed and ease in which she fell into this vicious cycle was staggering.

What happened with Poppy could happen to anyone, if there was no-one looking out for you. Luckily, through wisdom and a modicum of home discipline, my friends and I had enough savvy to see that path for what it was. The savagery and thoughtlessness of the world around her both cultivated and coveted her beauty but, at the same time, through jealously and ruthlessness, ripped it away from her and discarded her when it was no longer there. This is not too dissimilar to the effect on many elite athletes who were also seduced and then reduced. Taking drugs is like selling your soul. I saw it destroy people and, more pointedly, drugs kept people trapped within their own lonely and desolate existences.

A decade on from that, when television sports commentators questioned my behaviour towards fellow athletes in respect of drug taking, or maybe failed to comprehend my true stance on the moral position of drugs in sport, this was the background. I couldn't articulate it at the time, but with experience and hindsight, I can now appreciate that any association with drugs triggered anger within me. My view towards the scourge of drugs took a different path to others, despite us sharing exactly the same position. As a youngster I wanted no part of that world, and I wanted no part of it now that I was an athlete. In the same way that Mum's rule when I was a boy was to never bring police to the door, my rule as an adult was that nobody was ever to bring any performance-enhancing drugs within my circles, at all.

If people beat me – I wanted to understand and analyse why and how I was getting beaten. The driving force was not about winning, in itself, it was the process of working out how to win. The realisation that my purist approach to achieving self-fulfilment – in a world where those with a flexible approach to morals and rules appeared to reign supreme – was honourable but naïve, resulted in my inner demons being released. I had grown up among many who thought nothing of cheating and taking from others, and the response to such morals in a place like Moss Side was rage, retribution or resignation. Those who relied on those first two inevitably paid the price of personal pain, but in the world of track and field athletics the playing field was meant to be equal. I doubted that any drugs-cheat in sport experienced having a knock on the door in the early hours of the morning with a gang holding soaked petrol rags and blow torches asking them 'nicely' to play fair next time they competed. In many ways, therefore, the cheating and defrauding in athletics was done with less integrity and honour than on the streets. Sports cheats are not only fraudsters, but cowards.

With this disillusionment towards the fairness and sanctity of athletics, I had also always harboured ambitions of playing football. It wasn't a complete pipe dream. 'Multi-sport exposure' is a buzz phrase in academia and sporting commentary now, with the virtues of being multi-skilled in various disciplines very much in vogue. I was the very epitome of an individual enjoying multi-sport exposure while growing up in Sale. We played football on the field adjacent to my house for hours every night after school, as well as on weekends: pitching up at ten in the morning and playing until eight at night. It was one of the places that Mum used to drive past to discreetly check that we weren't misbehaving. My pace was an obvious asset but I had clearly been adept enough to have been invited to the Trafford School of Excellence alongside Ryan Giggs. The advent of the Premier League had made football a glamorous and aspirational sport to play, not just for the sizeable wage packets offered to players but also the impact of professionalism down to the leagues below which ensured that 'football athletes' became a term in itself. Most professional footballers during this period spent hours each day getting stronger and faster, and I was a ready-made physical specimen in this regard. Because of this, I became a viable option for trials at clubs and football became a real option for me. It wasn't a decision purely made by my ego, or as a two-fingered salute to track and field; I genuinely felt that I would regret it hugely if I didn't try and make the transition.

I had initially moved to Wales to train and live with Malcolm Arnold. His act of kindness towards me was life changing, and despite my best efforts to distance myself from my past, it kept creeping up on me. I thought that any remaining connections I had with Manchester's gang culture had gone, and that part of my life was behind me. However, one evening the police knocked on the door of the Arnold family home to question me about an incident. I felt awful that I had brought the police to Malcolm's door when they had given me a fantastic way of life that I had only seen on the television. They had cared for me like one of their own. I experienced plenty for the first time, and as a family they could not have made me feel more welcome or grateful. I even put on weight. I'd never seen so much fresh, homemade and baked food in my life – fruit, desserts and cakes – I was completely spoilt by the Arnolds and was also receiving the wisdom and benefit of probably the best coach in the world. I felt that I let Malcolm down, as well as myself.

I was falling out of love with athletics and I felt guilty for bringing aspects of my past into the sphere of people who had been exceptionally kind to me. During this time a very strange conversation occurred behind the scenes when I was injured and it struck a very raw nerve. I was told from a very surprising source that there were a few things that athletes could do to speed up the process of recovery from injury. As a relatively successful runner I was more than aware of these, I knew I could be more diligent in my preparation, post-exercise icing, recovery, and eating well.

I was corrected. No, there were *other* things that would allow me to recover quicker. There were many ways, I was told, that I could do it and 'nobody would know any different'. Whilst injured I could explore a few avenues that would help me get back stronger and quicker. The look of incredulity on my face in response must have shocked this person into silence, and we never discussed such things ever again when our paths crossed. The fact that this was brought into conversation in such a matter-of-fact way disturbed me greatly, for it was an indicator maybe of how overt and 'out-in-the-open' drugs could be spoken about. I also realised that the scourge of drugs could come from elite coaches (in many athletes' cases) or from the most unexpected of directions, in mine.

Track and I were like a long-term relationship that had become toxic. It had got to the stage where we brought each other no fun or enjoyment anymore. Every single reason or incident to justify leaving amplified the negativity and increased the case for walking away. Athletics had given me passion, discipline, values, respect, and taught me patience. However, while giving me all these things, it also gave me an opportunity for me to sell my soul, to cheat. I knew that at the top level there were many hushed conversations and many pointed fingers directed at certain individuals, but I was very naïve to its scale. I was the one with the murky background, yet I was now walking into a swamp which was darker and more sinister than Moss Side.

I had worn a cross on a necklace all my life, and it dawned on me that if I decided to sell my soul in this way, I couldn't wear the cross. It was one or the other, as I wasn't comfortable being a hypocrite. This was where my growing faith led me in the correct direction. I decided to quit athletics. Not temporarily. This was for good.

I was suddenly looking for a career, a job, and somewhere to live. I had met the footballer Nathan Blake while I was with Malcolm's training group, and I had integrated into his wide group of friends. Nathan was carving out a successful career for himself in the Premier League playing for Sheffield United, and I consulted with him about the realities of attempting to make it in the world of football. His close friends included his cousin Matthew Robinson, and another Commonwealth Games level sprinter Kevin Williams. Matthew was a talented athlete and ultimately won international rugby caps for Wales. There was a strong sporting theme running through this small group.

I briefly stayed with Matthew and then lodged with Kevin in the Ringland district of Newport. It was, and to a certain extent still is, a socially deprived and challenging area largely ignored by the politicians and ministers charged with improving such places. During the early 1990s, many of the post-war 'prefab' houses were still in existence as lived-in addresses. These pre-fabricated box houses made of wood, aluminium and in some cases asbestos, were designed to last a maximum of a decade, back in the mid-1940s, to replace the damage the Luftwaffe had left. In the St. Fagans National Museum of History, 15 miles away, these houses were presented as museum pieces, but sure enough in Ringland the original decade-long temporary solution for a housing shortage was still there half a century later, in various states of decay and dereliction.

Despite the feeling of the area being left behind and starved of investment, as exemplified by the towering presence of the Celtic Manor hotel complex being built on the adjacent hill like a lord's castle overseeing this proud working-class community, the people of Ringland were exceptionally warm hearted. It reminded me of Sale Racecourse in many ways and in that respect was a notice to me personally of how, despite my efforts to improve my lot, I was merely maintaining the social status quo for the Campbell family. I was labouring through temping jobs while trying my best to stay in shape in order to carve out a career in football, and I found myself working 12-hour shifts in the Tesco freezer section. The job made me respect the people who worked there, who were striving in order to pay the rent, to provide food on the table, or to enable them to afford their child's school trip. If you did your job properly nobody noticed you, but if you made a mistake you suddenly became visible. I learned the value of an honest day's work and the appreciation of how lucky I had been as a sportsperson in having such wonderful experiences all around the world.

During my time as an athlete I had been fortunate enough to have the financial help of Sir Eddie Kulukundis. He was a wealthy shipping and freight magnate whose philanthropic nature had ensured support for a huge number of aspiring British athletes. He had helped Denise Lewis, Linford Christie, Steve Ovett, Roger Black, and even supposedly paying the legal costs of Mo Farah's naturalisation as a British citizen. He had been a great help to me, but now having shunned athletics I was standing on my own two feet for the first time. It was scary.

I started playing Welsh league football for Ton Pentre and from there went on to Cwmbrân Town. That was a strange experience because Cwmbrân's stadium was also the track where I had often trained as an athlete. The domestic situation gave me a chance to establish my life in Wales outside of athletics, as well as providing a foundation for me to enjoy my football.

Being a semi-professional footballer, I looked for employment elsewhere in order to make both ends meet. Kevin Williams told me that there were potential opportunities in his line of work: insurance. So I went for an interview for a telesales role, but I was, in what I can only presume to have been an accident, offered a job handling insurance claims. Whether this was an error on their part or if they had seen something in my CV that led them to believe I could do this, I left the interview with a better job than the one I had applied for. However, the night before I was due to start this new role, while driving around the Newport area, I got lost around a McDonald's restaurant near the city centre. I was pulled over by the police who had obviously noticed that I was either lost, or acting suspiciously by weaving in and out of traffic looking for a way out. I was by now used to the fact I was also, as a black man doing the above, probably at an increased likelihood of being stopped.

While carrying out a routine check on the vehicle and my identity, the police officer's mannerisms and attitude kept changing the more information that was being relayed back through his earpiece, and I was asked to accompany him to the local station. I had absolutely no idea what was behind this request, but was told that Greater Manchester Police wanted to speak to me. I was put in the back of a police car – handcuffed, no less – and driven all the way up to Manchester. As soon as I got there, having checked all details and reviewing the evidence everyone realised that there had been an innocent misunderstanding which even rivalled the one in my job interview.

Apparently, a car had been used in some crime on the estate, and – of course – the perpetrators had not registered themselves as the vehicle's owners. The chances were that it had been stolen anyway. One of the previous owners was a Mr D. Campbell of Sale Racecourse estate hence my attendance at the police station. I was released immediately but I then had the rather uncomfortable task of telling my new employers that on the first day of my new job I was 200 miles away in a police station. I also had no transport, or money, to get back.

Luckily, fortune followed me around early in my football career. After playing a few games for Cwmbrân Town, a scout approached me and told me that he thought I had potential. He was the late Fred Edgington, a scout for a team back home in the north-west of England called Liverpool Football Club. He mentioned, sensibly, that there was a long career journey between Cwmbrân and Anfield, and that there was a lengthy chain between his recommendation and word reaching the manager. He could, however, arrange trials at a lower level and that is how I found myself playing for Millwall reserves against Arsenal, and a trial at Plymouth Argyle.

WILDERNESS

Fred Edgington soon became my agent and a friend, and by showing the skills I had, I found my level, which was non-league to semi-pro, maybe even League Two standard in today's English football pyramid. In my heart I knew I would never be as good a footballer as I was an athlete, but after that initial spell at football, as a bit of fun while working 9-5, I believed that moving up another level was within my grasp. Most managers noted the obvious advantage of my speed and work-rate, and having played the game for hours each day in my youth, I felt I had a decent positional awareness on the field. If someone played the ball over the top I was gone, but I didn't have the control from crosses, or didn't know how to utilise my speed specifically for football. The trial at Millwall didn't go well, though, as they played me on the right wing and my lack of positional awareness was fully exposed.

Prior to athletics I had played striker, and I felt that my physical abilities suited me more to that role than any other. I was offered a contract by Argyle, and played approximately ten games for the reserves, up until the period that Peter Shilton left the club as manager. If memory serves me right I scored around eight goals during that time and, as well as my on-field performances, I understood that being in favour with a manager was crucial for someone looking to build a career, both professionally and personally. Steve McCall eventually replaced Shilton as manager, and finding myself out of favour with the new boss at Argyle I moved to Weymouth FC as a semi-professional, where I played 27 games and scored four goals. When in Weymouth I stayed at the hotel owned by the club's chairman, Graham Carr, and recall being served breakfast each morning by Graham's young son, Alan, who progressed to serving up comedy for the entire country in a hugely successful career. Playing for 'The Terras' was fulfilling and I enjoyed my time there so it was a no-brainer when I was offered a semi-professional contract at around £200 per week.

This was above my basic pay at the time, and I signed it with relish. As fate would have it, the following day Neil Warnock, who had now replaced McCall as manager at Plymouth, called me on the recommendation of a scout; enquiring whether I would be interested in meeting him. Over his career, Warnock had a history of signing fast – Shaun Wright-Phillips – and physical – John Stead, Ade Akinbiyi – players, so maybe I struck a chord with his thinking despite coming from a track and field background, which he fully acknowledged wasn't an issue for him. It put me in a position of having to play the role of potential turncoat at Weymouth, especially considering that the ink on my contract was barely dry. The prospect of being considered to play professional football, however, was worth my knocking on the owner and manager's door. I was, in no uncertain terms, reminded that contracts go both ways (as they should, of course) and that they would see me for pre-season training. When things aren't meant to be, they aren't meant to be.

Sport can be brutal and ruthless. When you aren't offered a contract, it is done with a handshake and a pat on the back for good luck. One moment you are in, the next moment you are out in the cold. One final moment of joy was to come with Weymouth, at Wembley Stadium, in a race – held at half time during an England game – to find the fastest non-league footballer. Despite slipping at the start I took the title for the Terras, proudly wearing their shirt as I crossed the finish line. I would like to think that even if the league players had been included the result would have been the same. Through my football coaching I have encountered and worked with some exceptionally fast footballers. Adama Traoré was one I coached who had a genuine claim to be the world's fastest footballer, along with Gareth Bale. The difference between football fast and track fast, however, is measured in many metres.

Spells with what were then my local teams, Cwmbrân Town and Newport County, followed but the more I played the more I realised a stark truth. As a track athlete, I was in the top 1% in the UK. As a footballer, breaking into the top 15% was proving to be a challenge. I had no issue then, or now, in being so self-depreciatively realistic of my football exploits. Players and athletes at the top level excel precisely because they are excellent. Linford Christie won the 1995 British Championships, to be followed in subsequent years by Jason John and Toby Box, and as I was about to start a new season with Weymouth I kept on thinking, 'I used to beat those guys'.

My main rationale for leaving track and field was still sadly relevant, and I didn't regret walking away, but I had already half convinced myself of the decision to return to athletics. I started to think I would regret it if I didn't give sprinting one more shot.

5

Atlanta

*"She has lied for years. She treated everyone as idiots. I'm not shocked she
is going to jail. Many people criticised me because I was always the one
who lost in the Jones-Arron battle, even if I had very good results. She
has stolen my best years. Everything could have been different for me."*
Christine Arron, the French sprinter, on Marion Jones

A peer, and friend, Christine Arron of France, won 100m gold at
the European Championships in Budapest in 1998. Her comments
on how doping had directly impacted her career perfectly mirrored
mine, and encapsulated a large part of my motivation for leaving
the sport. We shared career paths not only in both winning our first
senior championship golds at the Europeans in Budapest, but also in
our values and principles. She was fed up with losing to cheats, and
I was overwhelmed by the size of the task in trying to compete with
them.

I felt that the tide of tainted medals not only diminished the glory
of the sport during the mid-1990s, but also severely diminished my
own personal hope that things would improve. Making sacrifices and
experiencing personal pain in pursuit of a goal was tough enough,
even with a level playing field, but if competing against what were –
at the time – relatively obvious dopers was the game we had to play,
I wasn't going to play it. This might have seemed an overly negative
and cynical take on the sport, but at the time the most successful
athletes – those winning the most medals and receiving the plaudits

and financial rewards – were the ones who were enveloped by doping scandals.

Marion Jones. Dwain Chambers. Kelli White. Tim Montgomery. Butch Reynolds. Justin Gatlin. Zhanna Pintusevich-Block. Anastasiya Kapachinskaya. Dennis Mitchell, Alvin Harrison and Antonio Pettigrew who, tragically, two years after being found guilty of doping was found dead in his car from an apparent suicide. It's a list as depressing in its quality as its length.

There was also an excessively high frequency of athletes pleading technicalities such as missed drug tests and offering alibis for their misdemeanours. Everywhere we looked as athletes – and as fans of the sport – the winners were being revealed as fraudsters with alarming regularity. It was a pretty depressing environment for clean athletes to exist in. The dopers were the ones succeeding, and frankly, at that time, they were all getting away with it. Even when authorities such as UKAD (UK Anti-Doping) or WADA (World Anti-Doping Agency) caught an athlete with a positive urine or blood sample, the legalities and processes required to punish the athletes in question were often lengthy and convoluted. Even to this day, many believe that the governing bodies of many nations protected their most famous athletes from the scrutiny of testing by turning a blind eye to failed tests. If this happened, a whole generation of athletes would have been effectively untouchable and protected by their own authorities – a practice that would be outrageous to suggest were it not so blatantly occurring in full view, even now.

There seemed to be a notion of 'two degrees of separation' in athletics during this time, where every single athlete knew someone who was part of a tainted training group, from a country with a system of doping, or knew their spouses and coaches were doping: everyone knew a someone with a question to answer. This eventually came to my door with people questioning Linford Christie's role as my coach. Some suggested there was a contradiction on my part, for protesting the values of a clean sport on one hand, but being associated with a banned athlete as a coach on the other. To clarify to those unaware of the situation and, more so, to reject any duplicity on my part when it came to doping, this was my take on the situation with Linford.

In 1999, having retired for two years as a sprinter and, crucially, having already taken on the mantle as my coach, Linford returned a positive test while running in a relatively meaningless indoor meet in Dusseldorf, Germany. He was then called to a hearing by the British Athletics Federation to provide evidence regarding this irregular sample. In this hearing, chaired by the BAF, he was cleared of wrongdoing. This came as a relief and I remember feeling grateful that his legacy as a world-class sprinter and one of Britain's best ever sportsmen would not be damaged. As an athlete under his tutelage, however, I was also relieved for not having to deal with the moral quandary of what to do if my coach was a proven drugs cheat.

This decision was later, and somewhat surprisingly, overturned by the IAAF. Another three UK athletes – Doug Walker, Mark Richardson and Gary Cadogan – shared the exact same fate: cleared by the BAF but pursued and sanctioned by the IAAF. They gave all the athletes, including Linford, a two-year suspension. According to the IAAF, their drug testing principle of 'strict liability on the part of the user' had not been applied by the BAF, thereby negating the opportunity to present a case beyond reasonable doubt that the drug was not taken deliberately. This was – for all four athletes – their primary defence: an inadvertent positive test resulting from cross-contamination from a legal supplement. Cross-contamination from other supplements was a regular occurrence during this time, before the athletic supplementation industry was more tightly regulated. This was caused because the huge industrial vats used to make protein powders and creatine tablets (all totally legal sporting aids) by a growing industry were also being used to make everything from animal feed to, in some cases, totally illegal supplements. The inevitable result of this practice was that people taking legal supplements were also, unbeknown to them, also taking microscopic but detectable amounts of banned substances. In this case, all the British athletes protested that they were taking exactly the same supplement which, according to the label of ingredients, was legal. That wasn't an excuse. That was a reason.

The problem with this defence was that, although it was morally valid for the truly innocent, it could be exploited as an obvious and ready-made alibi for those who were guilty of purposefully doping. As a result, despite almost certainly causing genuine 'false positives', it was easily waved away by cynics and the authorities alike. The contaminated supplements argument was met with significant smirking and eye-rolling at the time, particularly by the media, and to be fair, who could blame them?

However, the bottom line was that all the athletes in question had delivered positive test results, and their respective explanations for the adverse findings were accepted by their national body but rejected by the global authority. In Christie's case, the level of nandrolone in his system was so high as to be almost comedic. If the athletes in question were purposefully doping – especially Linford, whose result was off the scale – they shouldn't have because they were truly bloody awful at it. The IAAF re-instated Richardson, eventually, but Linford had already retired as a competitive athlete when was serving his ban, so he left his athletics career with this distasteful episode as its footnote.

Considering the fact that I had suffered losses at the expense of others, my stance on doping, and my eventual investment in a clean supplement company registered with Informed-Sport, I knew I had a lot to lose by being associated with a figure who'd been found guilty by the IAAF. I brought up the subject with Linford and, despite feeling that I didn't need to justify my association with him because he was my coach *prior* to the incident, I still felt then, as I do now, that I needed to validate my stance. So did he.

Linford was a polarising figure and people either loved him or loathed him. This polarisation still exists within the notion of the legacy he leaves as an athlete, as well as whether people believe his stance on the doping ban: he was awarded an OBE in 1998; sacked as a commentator by the BBC in 1999; had a statue built in honour of his 'B of the Bang' quotation in my home city of Manchester prior to the 2002 Commonwealth Games; was refused coaching credentials for the Olympic Games in 2000; yet inducted into the English Athletics Hall of Fame in 2010. All this, while still banned by the BOA (British Olympic Committee) as a coach, but still appointed as a mentor for athletes at the 2006 Commonwealth Games.

That appointment, in 2006, was objected to by Paula Radcliffe, who was not only one of Britain's best ever athletes, but also had a phenomenal and vocal track record in fighting doping. Paula knowingly suffered losses to dopers during her career, and her stance in this respect made her a respected figure, even without taking her remarkable sporting achievements into account. She took a credible moral stance against drugs, whereas mine was rooted in experience.

Yet, incredibly, even someone like Paula was farcically, and in an unsubstantiated way, indirectly named as a potential doper in a Parliamentary inquiry into blood doping. Using the convenient shield of Parliamentary privilege in 2015, MP Jesse Norman indirectly implicated Paula as having three 'suspect' test results. Having her name dragged through the court of public opinion, based on IAAF technicalities and differing conclusions by different sources, was grossly reckless. When challenged to substantiate such hugely damaging statements, the MP said it wasn't his intention to implicate anyone, calling into question the need to say anything in the first place. Thankfully, it was shown that there was no case to answer, but the greyness of the spectrum in which this information was presented, and by whom, created the false narrative that the achievements of one of the UK's finest athletes should be viewed with an element of suspicion. This is where I draw the parallel with Linford and myself. People were happy to shoot their mouths off without knowing the full story.

I know that one of Linford's greatest bugbears – which I shared, by the way – was that the same people preaching his defects were often doing so from decidedly shaky moral platforms themselves. Doping is one form of unfair competition, but so is bribery, nepotism, political manoeuvring and corruption. The sanctity of the sport depends on its cleanliness, yet the perception as to who is clean and who is tainted is often, sadly, a question of trust and public persona as much as it is reliant on evidence. Linford will always be far too abrasive to win that battle. To quote *Guardian* journalist Andy Bull, Christie's case wasn't given much slack because, 'he was seen as something of an asshole'. It was this personality-driven bias against what should have been a clear scientific case of 'did he or didn't he' that forced me to look at the issue from a different angle. The fact that neither UK Athletics nor the IAAF could agree for any of the four athletes' cases clouded it even further. As a self-appointed flag bearer of clean athletics, I could have easily used this to my advantage in joining the sanctimonious finger-wagging brigade, but knowing these four athletes – Christie, Cadogan, Richardson and Walker – the way I did, or at least I thought I did, I decided not to score that open goal. I allowed, and will allow, history to make its own judgement, without virtue-signalling along the way. So, it was in this spirit that I chose to believe Linford in 1999 when it was necessary for me to make a choice.

I had lost personal motivation for the sport partly through the realisation that the deceit and injustice that occurred within it conflicted hugely with my love for athletics. There was further conflict in the fact that athletics as a sport had played a central part in helping my social mobility from a previous existence of injustice and deprivation. The dream I had set when I was younger – the one I had told my primary school teachers about – had gone. I had told Mr Law at school, Mum and Lynx that I was going to be the next Carl Lewis, and not the next Gullit or Van Nistelrooy.

As my football escapades wound down, I believed I could succeed further in athletics despite the challenges of the previously uneven playing field. Achieving success in team sports demanded talent and the ability to play a role within a team. It also demanded being content for your talent to be judged subjectively by coaches, managers and directors. Ultimately, in team sports you are chosen to represent a team. In athletics, however, if you ran close to ten seconds for the 100m, whether in Cwmbrân or Cupertino, you would be invited to Diamond League races the following week. In an individual sport like track and field I could truly be the master of my own destiny if I was good enough, so I decided to set aside ten months to train, and see if I could once again get close to top level sprinting. In late 1995 I competed at what was slowly becoming my multi-sport 'home' track of Cwmbrân Stadium (when in truth I was still, in mind and body, a footballer), and had posted a very respectable time of 10.34. It was a good first step and placed me in a strong position to get back to the top.

I gave my agent, Sue Barrett, a call and told her that I was thinking of returning to athletics. I asked her if she could speak with Linford to ask if I could train with him. Linford was the Olympic 100m champion at this point, preparing to defend the title he'd won at Barcelona at the forthcoming Atlanta Games. I couldn't think of anyone finer to train with, not only in order to help propel me back into top level athletics, but also as a future mentor.

It was a shock, and a chastening one at that, when Linford said no. He didn't believe I was serious, and also that my approach wasn't earnest enough. He referenced points in the past where I had allowed distractions to get in the way. Essentially, if I hadn't been serious enough in the past why should he believe was I serious now? I fully understood his initial reaction. After all, here I was – a retired athlete, come retired footballer – assuming I could slot straight into the training group of a reigning Olympic champion.

Yet, with the help of a few sponsors, and an introduction from Linford himself, I was sent to Germany to see the famed doctor Hans-Wilhelm Müller-Wohlfahrt in order to get a full physical check-up. I had been suffering from hamstring issues for a while, both as an athlete and footballer, and he identified a tilt in my pelvis as a possible cause of the problem, potentially caused by a minor car crash I had been involved in as a youngster. After several manipulations and injections into my back I was given the thumbs up and was ready to start training again. As a fantastic bonus, Linford had had a change of heart. I was back in his group.

Our training partners were Colin Jackson, Jamie Baulch and Paul Gray. Linford was always a very tough trainer, who stressed the need for strength rather than speed and endurance. We used 120m and 130m sprints in order to have that closing speed endurance in the latter stages of a race, while Jamie, as a longer sprinter, was doing 300s and 400s. We worked very hard alongside Linford, who was also highly motivated to retain his Olympic title.

We used the gym in the Welsh Institute of Sport at Sophia Gardens (now the home of Sport Wales), and the track at Leckwith (now redeveloped as the Cardiff City Stadium) for everything else. The relationship we had with the staff at Leckwith was fantastic. We became very close and they even gave us a set of keys so that we could use the track during off-times and over Christmas. They were always very supportive of us.

The training leading up to the Atlanta Olympics was very much a 'suck it and see' approach for me. I had an intention to return to the top, and a clear personal drive to do so, but I'd just returned to the sport so my own expectations weren't weighing heavily on me. The Olympics were being held in July and August 1996, which meant I would have to perform well at the British trials in late June in order to qualify. I ran 10.17sec at Bratislava in my first race that season and was very happy with my return as a competitive athlete. At the Amateur Athletic Association (AAA) Championship that season, which acted as the Olympic trials, I finished fourth in a time of 10.30 which made me a potential pick for the 4 x 100m relay team. I had told myself that unless I finished in the top three in the trials, I didn't deserve to go to any major championship, but because the relay team needed a larger squad to get through the qualifying rounds my fourth-place finish may have been good enough. This ended up being the case, and fresh from returning to athletics, I was on the way to my first Olympics.

Elite athletics is a serious business because you are only one weak session away from making yourself slower, or worse, getting yourself injured. Most athletes know the perils of not focusing on the small, marginal details and I'm certainly not aware of any other sport that requires everyone to 'switch on' mentally as often and as frequently. When races and championships came, my level of concentration took on a whole new dimension. Having learned from seeing Linford, off-track, metamorphasizing into Linford, on-track, every sinew of my being became the person that people would watch on television: the intense 1,000-yard stare with steely, lifeless eyes, and the biting of lips like a warrior preparing for battle. At that moment, not a single distraction would enter my head. I would have my own mental 'triggers' to maintain concentration, whether they be biting on my necklace or clenching my fists. This, to me, was all a part of the act of stepping into character. I needed, through my mannerisms and body language, to reflect the seriousness of the occasion. Nothing would be allowed to distract from my creation of the aura of resolute determination to succeed.

Until the era of Usain Bolt, this would be the adopted persona of most athletes. In the pre-Bolt world of track and field, where the difference between first and fifth was often miniscule – as opposed to the much more significant margins, which could be measured in metres, when Usain ran – solemn concentration was the default pre-race setting for most athletes, not the mock combing of hair, flirting with the girls or pointing at the television audiences at home. Bolt could get away with this, such was his dominance. For me, focus and solemnity went hand in hand.

Yet, we all have our lapses, and for a period leading up to the Atlanta Olympics my default setting blew a fuse. I wasn't focused on running as much as I should have been. I had trained hard to get to a stage where I was no longer a footballer and was now an athlete again, and simply the act of succeeding with that transition constituted success. The Olympic experience, in all its grandiose pomp, blew me away. The celebration of the event (in true American style) was full of razzmatazz and I soaked up every minute of the joy of being a part of the greatest sporting celebration on earth. I felt privileged to be there, but it also filled me with an arrogance that, by being there, I had 'made it' as an athlete. I had forgotten to focus on the opportunity when it was given. Being talented and physically prepared was only one part of the jigsaw, and without an anchor keeping me grounded I was doomed to underachieve. The 1996 Olympics, in that respect, was a master class in naivety, and of a failure to deal with external distractions. Maybe my ego – knowing that only nine months since quitting football I found myself at the peak of top level athletics – had got the better of me. Elite sport, in its own inimitable way, decided to remind me that the weather is always windier and harsher at the exposed top of the mountain, and I left those Olympics with my tail somewhat between my legs.

We had a training and holding camp in Gainesville, Florida (home of the Florida Gators), with Linford's group, and despite my promises about returning to athletics as a mature, focused sportsman, this is when I began to take my eye off the ball. I had left athletics as a junior and returned as a senior, but I still had the mentality of a junior athlete, with the immature antics, partying and late nights. That mentality, when combined with the Olympic Village was a dangerous mix. It is an amazing place, full of people from all around the world where an eclectic vibe exists among like-minded people. Most sportspeople have a dream of going to the Olympics, but only a small percentage win medals at each Games. Each competitor embarks on a different quest: many had already achieved their life's goal by getting to the Olympics and were there for the experience, to enjoy themselves and revel in the environment. I didn't think I was one of those people, but I found myself as one once I was there. The whole Olympic experience came too quickly and too easily for me, before I was mature enough to appreciate the opportunity.

The Atlanta Olympic Village had a nightclub, bars, and fast-food outlets – all the attractions you wouldn't expect to coexist with the quest to be 'faster, higher and stronger'. For some, especially after finishing their events, their Olympic motto became 'later, drunker, tired'. I didn't fall into this trap, but I certainly got caught up in the euphoria of 'Wow! I'm at the Olympic Games'. Our accommodation was quite far from the centre of the village so we had to take a bus to the food hall, and the buses always seemed to be full. Each team's VIPs, such as the *chef de missions*, had the use of golf buggies which seemed unfair, so a few athletes that must remain nameless – and might, or might not, have included yours truly – learned how to hotwire these buggies for their own use. It was harmless japery but it was somehow symbolic of the light-hearted attitude a few of us had of our Olympic journey. The bombing, at the start of the Games during a concert at the Centennial Olympic Park, had tragically killed two people, and the resultant security around the village created an unreal, insulated, bubble-type scenario. The bomb also created a level of fear among the athletes which, for many I'm sure, resulted in an enhanced feeling of camaraderie within our secure environment, which superseded competitive instincts.

In the meantime, back at the sharp end, things were going smoothly with our relay practice. We were aware of the chequered history of the British relay team, not only in terms of success but also in the feat of getting the baton all the way around the track. We were determined to not let complacency, or carelessness, impact our challenge for medals. It felt like I was fifth or sixth in the pecking order for the relay, so I wasn't very confident that I'd have the opportunity to run, and thought – just like the World Championships in 1993 – I was there for the experience and as a back-up runner as opposed to being a starter. So when I was told the night before the heats that I was running the following day, I was not mentally prepared. I got very nervous and I didn't sleep at all. That one night felt like three days.

Race day dawned and I emerged, after a sleepless night, from the depths of the stadium into a noisy cauldron of partisan and very hostile Americans. I think, at one point, we might even have been booed. It was very hot, humid and sticky, and the lack of sleep made the whole experience rather surreal: like an out-of-body experience. As a quartet, we were aware that we were outsiders for a podium finish, but this was never publicly expressed or even admitted, for the body language and the positive talk always had to be about the quest for gold. Even accounting for that realistic mindset, the disappointment of missing out on the final was unexpected, and emotionally crushing.

We crashed out in the heat in farcical circumstances. It had been a complete disaster, and I was a big part of it. It held greater significance for one of the four athletes who would have been in the final. Throughout his career, Linford had never left a major championship empty-handed, yet due to my own hands being empty and baton-less upon leaving the relay exchange box on the final bend, we were about to deliver that to him, with a cherry on top. The mistake was a simple one; Darren Braithwaite and I had practised our timings meticulously prior to the race itself but I miscalculated my start and had to put on the brakes – otherwise we would have been disqualified for exchanging the baton outside the legal zone. As it happens, this kind of error is enough to make the other teams whizz past you in such a way that you had might as well be disqualified anyway. The British team's baton ended up travelling at great speeds, but not in the hand of any athlete. I launched it across the track in exasperated frustration as I saw the other teams race away towards qualification for the final.

There are many reasons behind such public howlers in a closed skill like a baton exchange in a sprint relay, but the primary reason often lies within the minds of those tasked with executing it. Had I got nervous? Had my anxiety at being desperate to show my ability to shine at the highest stage played a part in my jumping the gun? I've no doubt that even though I lay the blame solely at my own feet, Darren Braithwaite also probably searched his own thoughts for reasons on why it went so wrong. Even to this day, the seconds surrounding that exchange are still a blur of what I think happened, and what truly happened. The fact is that over 20 years after the incident, there is still no mental clarity for me. That itself may be a strong indicator of why it happened in the first place. The moment and the situation provided confusion when there was a need for clarity.

One of the first people I saw afterwards was Denise Lewis. Denise was an idol of mine. She won a bronze medal in the heptathlon at the Atlanta Games and would be Olympic champion in Sydney four years later. The required empathy and sympathy that crashing out of an Olympic dream was non-existent in our brief encounter: "You're a fucking disgrace you are."

Being a talented and driven athlete herself, she could see right through the people that were cutting the corners and denying themselves the full investment in their talents. People like me. Her comment stabbed me in the heart: one of my heroes and idols dressing me down immediately after the fall. The fact was, however, she was absolutely right. I took it all – the Olympics, my ability, the gift I had been given, for granted. I needed to realise where I was and change things. People like Denise Lewis could see me for what I was. I just wished, for a few precious seconds, that maybe I had succeeded as a footballer.

It was a humid and sticky day on 3 August 1996, when Marva Campbell was on her way to work and slowly navigating her way through Piccadilly Station in Manchester. During the morning rush-hour, the pace and rhythm of the station was frantic as everyone jostled and pushed their way to their trains. Marva was in a hurry, but her legs almost gave way as she walked past one of the newsagents. The warmth and frivolity of the bustling station vanished into the background as her gaze was immediately fixed on the front pages of the papers. Her son's face was plastered everywhere in a picture of howling anguish. Her son had been chosen by editors up and down the country to be that day's poster boy for failure. There had been another British failure at the Olympics – this time in the relay – and it was my fault.

6

Budapest

"For that, Linford, not only am I going to win gold but I am going to take your championship record with it."

The decision to return to athletics felt as natural as was the decision to leave. It felt right to walk away at the time, and it felt right to come back. The realisation that I was an athlete and not a footballer was self-evident. My motivation to return had always been to prove something to myself, and also to those who were adamant that success in athletics could only be achieved by taking short cuts. I had enjoyed my brief time in football, and the dynamic of existing within a true team sport was one that I felt served me well when I went into coaching a few years later. The experience at the Atlanta Olympic Games, however, had been a wake-up call. I had gone from being an athlete that certain sections of the population had heard of, to being infamous for being 'that guy' who had dropped the baton. I needed to change that label, and change it quickly.

A source of personal redemption came a few months later when the IAAF Grand Prix Final was held in Milan, in early September. The president of the IAAF, Primo Nebiolo, had insisted that a major track and field meet was to be held in Sarajevo, the war-torn capital of Bosnia and Herzegovina, two days afterwards. The meet was called Solidarity in Sarajevo and the idea was that many of the world's leading athletes would be flown from Milan to Sarajevo to compete in an event which would symbolically raise the profile and the morale of the city.

Sarajevo had been under siege from Bosnian Serbs since 1992, and in September 1996 the atmosphere there was still tense, despite the war having officially ended with the signing of the Dayton Agreement in December 1995. This would be the first major sporting event to be held in the country since war had broken out in the former Yugoslavia almost five years earlier. Nebiolo was using his significant influence as the head of a world sporting governing body to, apparently, create some good. There was no other agenda.

Nebiolo's dream, however, was turning sour. One by one, many of the world's best athletes found their reasons, or their excuses, for not travelling to Sarajevo. Athletes who had competed at the Milan Grand Prix final two days earlier found themselves suddenly unable to attend. Michael Johnson, Jonathan Edwards and Noureddine Morcelli had all been lauded and courted by Nebiolo as figureheads of the event, but Johnson decided against going after consulting with, among others, the United States Embassy. Edwards announced that he had never confirmed his presence at the event in the first place and therefore didn't attend, while Morceli had strangely contracted flu since the Milan meet two days earlier. Dennis Mitchell, the American sprinter, was reported as saying that athletics was his life, but not worth his life. Nebiolo could hardly contain his disgust: "Some athletes have shown that they are not brave," he stated in a thinly-veiled riposte. His noble effort to create solidarity with the people and city was in danger of achieving quite the opposite. It signalled to the people of Sarajevo that the world simply wasn't ready to stand side-by-side with them quite yet.

The journey to Sarajevo was long. As soon as we arrived at the airport it was clear that things here were far from normal. The terminal building was a wreck. We were shepherded into buses by armed guards, and the bus ride to the hotel itself was sobering. Any notion of complaining about the lack of luxuries and niceties was immediately quashed as we drove past miles upon miles of bomb-devastated buildings, riddled with bullet holes, and with plastic sheets for windows. At every turn there were signs warning of the dangers of landmines and the whole place was like a museum of human suffering on a grand scale. The bus fell completely silent. It was humbling enough to think that some people were living in these conditions, but the truth was worse. There wasn't anyone around who *wasn't* living in these conditions. Many of the athletes wept.

BUDAPEST

During the journey into the city we were given a sombre commentary on the scenery around us, including on the significance of the red resin marks – dubbed Sarajevo Roses – on most of the buildings which were remnants of the mortar shell explosions. Upon arrival at the hotel, we were briefed by a United Nations commander who advised us all to stay away from all grassy areas as there was still a very real threat from landmines. I remember chatting to a local athlete who commented that even the sound of the starter's pistol would be an unpleasant reminder of the conflict to all 50,000 spectators present in the stadium that day.

The meeting was held at the Koševo Stadium in Sarajevo, the location of the opening ceremony of the 1984 Winter Olympics, and the event was the symbolic reopening of the Olympic Stadium, the rebuilding of which had been partly funded by the IAAF. Adjacent to the stadium, in what was now a crumbling wreck of concrete, bullet holes and mortar shells, was the arena where Torvill and Dean had skated their way to gold, ice-dancing to Ravel's *Bolero*. This brought back poignant memories to me of watching that competition on television back home in Manchester. The Koševo Stadium itself was still surrounded by sand-bags, NATO troops, and barbed wire. The event and the performances themselves were an irrelevance. We were there to show camaraderie. I was proud that I made the journey to Sarajevo, and had paid respects to the city in a time of need. Once I had decided to attend, I was not going to go back on my word and join the bandwagon of those seeking an excuse for their absence.

I felt a huge sense of pride, and sadness, in leaving the stadium. Local children held our hands and smiled through eyes that had seen things no child should ever see. My overwhelming feeling was that the athletes who had pulled out – in some cases stating some rather melodramatic fears over their safety – had missed out on a life-affirming experience by doing so. Was it dangerous there? Of course, but a bomb had exploded and killed people in Atlanta a few weeks earlier yet no athletes felt a need to withdraw from that event.

Nebiolo and the UN had a lot to lose if any incidents occurred in Sarajevo and, in reality, there was nothing but goodwill on both sides. It would have meant so much to the Sarajevo residents who had experienced such harrowing evil and pain for so many years to see some of their heroes in the flesh. I do believe that some of the glamorous 'world's bests' that track and field lauded at the time, had truly missed out. They would have learnt so much from the residents of Sarajevo in terms of humility, self-awareness and love for their fellow man. Letting go of the children's hands outside the stadium, as they pleaded for us to stay, reduced me to tears. It made me wonder what the future held for them. We athletes had only been asked to be there for two days, whereas many of the children had lived through hell their whole lives.

As athletes, there would be plenty of opportunities for competitive one-upmanship in the months and years following the Solidarity in Sarajevo meeting. Many of us who had made the journey to Sarajevo felt a palpable sense of how lucky we were to be able to leave such a place and carry on with our lives. In future competitions, for those who chose to be absent, there could be no more bravado, no more pre-race attempts at intimidation and no more aggressive posturing. The chance to demonstrate their public fortitude and character had come, and gone. Even those blessed with a golden touch on the track could simultaneously be afflicted by a touch of yellow off it.

We all have our challenges in life and our own internal character conflicts, however, and I was no way immune to these. I had by this time become rather too familiar with casinos, and I would often combine the multiple vices of late nights with risking my hard-earned money over the roulette tables. I was living in Ringland with Kevin, and it is probably fair to say that I had picked up a gambling habit. It was far from being an addiction, but it was becoming an interest that I enjoyed a little too much. One night, while I was in a casino in Cardiff, a young lady caught my attention. I had become familiar with some of the staff and doormen and enquired about who she was and sent the signals out as discreetly as I could. As the night wore on, I noticed that she had been at a table, alone, so I approached her and introduced myself. We started talking, got on well, and before we knew it, we realised that we had been talking for hours. When the casino closed around 4am, we left together and walked the streets of Cardiff, talking until the sun came up over the Welsh capital. When the inevitable tiredness hit us both, I kissed her on the cheek, bade her farewell and that was it. Her name was Clair, and she was from the Ely district of the city.

Almost immediately we started dating. Clair initially had no idea that I was an athlete, and within weeks of meeting each other we had a serious hurdle to overcome in an athletic sense: I was about to travel to Australia for three months to take part in a training camp. Despite the fact that I was very eager for us to keep seeing each other, any decision not to go would be hard to justify seeing as how our relationship was only three weeks old. I wanted her to wait for me, but it was a big thing to ask of her. I went so far as to tell a friend of mine that if we successfully made it through this period I was going to marry her. Before this I hadn't been ready to settle down, but meeting Clair made it crystal clear to me that I was.

Athletics was my first love, but since meeting Clair everything had changed, so if she was willing to wait, I would make sure that it would be worth both our whiles. In Australia, I stayed up until all hours of the morning but this time, instead of partying I was talking to Clair on the phone. With the time difference and her work commitments, it became an exercise in logistics. When I returned, I was met with a huge mobile phone bill. The 90-minute phone calls, each night, for ten weeks, over 11,000 miles, meant that I had run up a bill over £4,000. It would have been cheaper to fly Clair over on business class. After the initial shock of the phone bill I began to view it as a wise financial investment in my future.

The Australia trip was a training camp designed to prepare us for the 1997 World Athletics Championships in Athens. Despite running well in the heats, I failed to make the 100m final. I had decided that I didn't want to run in the relay because dropping the baton in Atlanta was still a stone in my shoe. There had been no support since that incident from any quarter, and I was left to deal with the personal trauma, the newspaper headlines and the innuendos alone. I also felt that despite Britain being relatively well blessed with a depth of sprinters – such as Darren Braithwaite, Julian Golding, Doug Walker, Dwain Chambers and Marlon Devonish – there was little structure, little guidance and little evidence of team spirit. It felt as if we were set up for a fall, and I didn't want to be in such a situation again. To compound things even further, one of the UK's most consistent sprinters that season, Ian Mackie, suffered an injury and I was placed in a situation where the decision to run was taken out of my hands.

The performances proved that there was a disconnect between presumption and behaviour. We won our heat, showing exceptional fluidity in the baton changeovers, and received the boost that the

USA had failed to finish their heat so were therefore out of the competition. In the final we surpassed all our expectations in winning a very creditable bronze. To me, this highlighted the importance of focusing on the here and now, in the knowledge that external forces and historical behaviours could play a part, or not, if you allowed them to.

When I returned home, bolstered with a World Championship medal, more important things needed my immediate attention. Clair and I decided to get a place together in Pontprennau, a new-build suburb on the eastern side of Cardiff. At that time my income and financial security from athletics was not sufficient for me to have real control over any long-term family situation, but further success in athletics was certainly a way to attain it.

Soon after getting back from Athens, settling into our new home and catching a breath, it was time for off-season training again. The winter of 1997 was a gruelling one, but I had an extra spring in my step having met Clair. Our training group was on the top of its game, and Jamie and I relocated to Namibia for a dose of warm-weather training. It seemed that we were all pushing each other and – for reasons that sometimes you can't put your finger on – we were all demanding much more of one another while also getting closer as a crew. In Namibia we stayed with the sprinting legend Frankie Fredericks, who opened up his home to us and was, as always, exceptionally kind and benevolent. This was, and still is, one of the paradoxical natures of top-level track and field. Rivals on the track would train with each other and motivate one another in order to achieve better standards with the goal of being able to beat the other in competitions. We trained at altitude and it felt like breathing through a straw. At times I would wake up in the middle of the night, short of breath. The stopwatch never lies, however, and we were elevating our standards while also enjoying each other's company. Despite the arduous physical nature of training, I remember being truly happy with a warm glow of positivity and feeling constantly upbeat.

Athletics was the foundation of my persona, and my sporting ambitions, but how would it cope with family life? This notion was put to the test when Clair discovered she was pregnant. The summer of 1998 was to be the one that would define the real start of my athletics career, with the European Championships and then the Commonwealth

Games in Kuala Lumpur on the horizon. Clair made the astonishingly selfless decision of keeping the news of her pregnancy from me for a brief period in order for me to concentrate on the last few weeks of the track season. She had obviously considered all eventualities, and being as petite as she is, it would be impossible for her to conceal her condition. It must have been a difficult decision for her to delay informing me of our wonderful news: a decision, I'm sure, based on her knowledge of how I would deal with the information. I was gaining in maturity, but I still had a selfish ruthlessness when it came to my goals. Put simply, she just didn't want to distract me until the time was right.

As a young athlete, I was notoriously low on self-control and was emotionally impulsive. Through a combination of rashness and a short temper, I could easily shoot myself in the foot at any given opportunity. The challenge ahead of me was to apply some maturity and self-awareness into my preparation and performances. The red mist had a nasty habit of coming down, and others knew it. I thought selfishness coupled with a determination would lead to greater achievement in sport, so I concentrated completely on myself and my own goals. In fact I only realised how self-absorbed I was when I retired, and when the extra time and energy that I had to focus on relationships, other people and family became apparent.

Without a doubt, the experiences at Sarajevo had made me evaluate the futility of bravado and posturing, and in my mid- to late-20s I finally learned to be aware of, if not control, my instincts. In other words, I grew up. I can vividly remember the moment that the negative effect of my short fuse and poor self-control revealed themselves to me. It was in Budapest at the 1998 European Athletics Championships. All the physical pre-requisites were present for me to succeed in Hungary. I had trained well and was in really good shape. I was in a position to win medals and both my coach, Linford Christie, and I knew it.

Paul Gray, Colin Jackson, Jamie Baulch and me had been challenging each other to greater things over the winter and there was a feeling that we were on to something special. Paul had run well in his first heat of the 400m hurdles, posting a time which would have been close to a medal in the final, but narrowly missed out as a fastest loser in the semi-final. Jamie was a part of the 4 x 400m relay squad which won gold – breaking the magical three minute barrier – and Colin took the gold once again in the 110m hurdles. It seemed that I had been training every day with a crew of athletes who were primed for exceptional performances on the big stage.

The championships were held at the Népstadion (The People's Stadium) in Budapest, which was to be renamed later as Puskás Stadium after the legendary Hungarian footballer Ferenc Puskás. This was a stadium steeped in history, as a multi-sport area – it was where the England football team suffered their worst-ever defeat, 7-1, in 1954 – and as a concert venue hosting performers such as U2, the Rolling Stones and Queen. I was hoping, of course, to create my own history.

The logistics of competing through various rounds of sprint competitions in major championships involved two heats that were usually both on the same day, and then semi-finals and finals the following day with a short break of a few hours between them. After the second round of heats I was the quickest qualifier, but as I was preparing for my semi-final Linford approached me with a beaming smile on his face and a bounce in his step. In 1998 he was effectively retired as an athlete and was coaching us more than competing himself. He came to the pre-race warm-up area where I was receiving a pre-race mobility massage from my friend, the late John Sales. Dwain Chambers had run a quicker time in his semi-final than I had ever achieved in my entire career up to that point. He ran just over 10.1 on what was, by the evidence from the results in both men's and women's events, a track not predisposed to quick times. Linford was excited and emotional, eager to relay to me, with a level of passionate incredulity, the quality of Dwain's performance: "Did you see what Dwain just did?" He beamed enthusiastically, "Dwain just looked absolutely awesome."

Linford knew my weakness. He knew my impulsive anger and weak self-control. He proceeded to double down on waxing lyrical about my rival by commenting on how impressive he looked, even suggesting how he was primed for something special for the final. By this point the tension was becoming unbearable and my blood pressure was rocketing. I was either being challenged by Linford, or goaded, but in attempting to do this he was running the risk that I would get impulsive and emotional. This heightened arousal and anger would trigger my notoriously poor self-control and it would almost certainly negatively affect my performance. I rarely needed a 'gee-up', if anything I needed a jockey to pull back on the reins.

BUDAPEST

I felt that I was in a position to win the European title yet, merely an hour before the final, felt my old demons returning. This was all because of Linford. I needed to compose myself and this was when the awareness of needing to stay calm dawned on me for the first time. I was suddenly hugely aware that my lack of self-control was a threat to success. I turned to Linford, with a smile: "For that, Linford, not only am I going to win gold but I am going to take your championship record with it" (Christie being the holder of the quickest time at the European Championships in the men's 100m).

I continued with my massage, and as John rubbed me and stretched me, I became aware that he too had become nervous and edgy following Linford's comments. I had maintained my composure but my masseur, of all people, had become tense. I could feel his nerves being transmitted to me so I instructed him to take a five-minute break; go for a stroll and return to me when he felt he could be as relaxed as I had become. John, poor guy, must have thought, 'who is this and what have they done to the Darren Campbell I know?' This level of composure was not what he was used to. He must have expected me to blow a fuse after Linford's comments, and his edginess was probably rooted in the confusion he felt towards my calmness. For the first time in my career, and only moments before my semi-final, I learned not only the value of self-control but also acknowledged that therein lay my weaknesses. If I couldn't own my self-control, people were going to exploit the lack of it. Dwain was supremely confident and was good enough to win; however, in that race I probably demonstrated the greatest amount of self-belief and control in my entire career up to that point.

There were three Brits in the final; Dwain, Marlon and me. I can recall feeling very calm – with almost no nervous energy – prior to the call to the blocks, as if I was sub-consciously suppressing any anger that the winding-up from Linford should have generated. As the gun fired, and as we all rose from our crouched positions to be in full stride, I realised I was out in front with the Greek athlete Papadias on my right shoulder and running well. It was at this point that I expected the field to pull away and for the fight to begin for medals. Then, a little after halfway, I sensed that both Dwain and me were starting to create some daylight between us and the other six runners. The reality that most people might not be aware of, is that sprinters do not accelerate and then keep getting quicker all the way to the line. Most reach a peak speed at around 50 metres and then slow down gradually as fatigue hits. The winner is often the athlete that slows down the least. This is a part of the scientific approach to sprinting that justifies the overspeed and speed endurance work done in winter months. Dwain and I had reached peak speed and were cruising nicely at 50 metres.

A second scientific concept, which every sprinter who runs a straight line can relate to, is Einstein's theory of relativity and, bizarrely as it sounds, this played a part in my Budapest win. I felt time slow down enough for me to gather my thoughts. Despite the race only lasting ten seconds, the quicker we travelled the more thinking time we had to appraise and to evaluate. My thoughts briefly wandered, and I began contemplating whether, if the winter endurance and strength work I'd soldiered through were going to give me any spur at all, this would be it. It was a sprinter's equivalent of the pause a racing-car driver experiences before changing down gear and accelerating to overtake an opponent.

Sure enough, with 30 metres to go I felt a wind hit my sails and I maintained my speed as others were starting to slow down. I raised my arm as I crossed the line – without dipping –in the full knowledge that I was European Champion. The next ten seconds became a blur: the realisation of a dream and the rather underwhelming feeling of, 'What am I meant to feel like now?' It was my first senior title in athletics and the immediacy of it felt the same as finishing a British League event in Croydon. I held my face in my hands and tried to take it all in. I'm sure Paul Gray and Jamie Baulch posted personal bests as they sprinted past the on-track security to mob me on the bend. Celebrating with training partners was half the joy of success, and in embracing my fellow training partners the wave of euphoria hit me. I had also made good on my promise to Linford – I took his European Championship record in the process.

During his television commentary on the race, the brilliant and greatly missed David Coleman accidentally called me Dwain Campbell – one of his infamous 'Colemanballs' – but as I had won my first senior individual title he could have called me anything and I would have forgiven him for it.

Britain ultimately topped the medal table at the Games. All the men's sprint titles (100m, 200m and 400m) were won by Britain, and Team GB won nine golds in total. Allyn Condon, Julian Golding,

Dougie Walker and I also won gold in the 4 x 100m relay to cap a highly memorable European Championships, and 1998 was a high point for British athletics. It was also a pretty important year for Clair and me. The question was, would this act as a springboard for further success or was there another bump in the road on the way? If previous history acted as the best predictor of future performance, it could have gone either way.

I had watched Iwan Thomas' magnificent performance in winning the 400m title – breaking the championship record in the process – but I had missed the semi-finals of his event (as most athletes take a passing interest in the earlier rounds, even if their teammates are involved, they will of course be there to cheer them on in finals). Within those semi-finals occurred an event of great significance for me but it wouldn't reveal itself until Sydney two years later. A largely unknown Greek athlete had failed to qualify for the final of the 400m which led him to re-evaluate his best distance as a sprinter. His name was Konstantinos Kenteris.

7

Sydney

"Don't worry, by the morning your silver will be gold."

The gold in Budapest made me European 100m champion, and winning such titles do put an extra spring in one's step – a very useful trait to have as a sprinter. Yet being European champion didn't immediately catapult me on to better things, as the 1999 World Championships held in Seville proved. I missed the 100m final by 0.01 of a second and I didn't qualify for the 200m.

It was an underwhelming World Championships for the British team – Colin Jackson, in the 110m hurdles, won our only gold — which finished below Romania, Spain, Morocco and Greece in the medal table. As we prepared for the 4 x 100m relay final you could sense that the aeroplane engines were already 'good to go' to get the team home. It was time to write the season off and start again.

The quartet of Jason Gardener, Marlon Devonish, Dwain Chambers, and me, ran well in a very smooth display of baton-passing and finished second behind the Americans, but our silver felt like scant consolation at the end of a bad day. We had finished a mere 0.14 of a second behind the gold medallists but our performance fell well under the radar and attracted little attention from our peers or from the press, despite being a new European record. There was no celebration or plaudits for what, even to this day, was a bloody good silver medal performance from an up-and-coming British quartet. As history would prove, three of us who ran that day would be crowned Olympic champions five years later in Athens. Everything starts somewhere.

SYDNEY

My family had also started. Our beautiful first son, Aaryn, was born in 1999, and having such a precious gift added to the sense that Clair and I were on the right track. I had two golds and a silver from senior athletics championships, but none could compare to the feeling of being a father for the first time. I had a passion for athletics, and now I also had a mission to be a devoted, compassionate and attentive father – the very things I'd been deprived of as a boy. Aaryn was a good-looking baby – an attribute he clearly inherited from his mother – who the midwives at the hospital couldn't stop doting over. Poor Clair had endured a torrid 36-hour labour, and while her easily distracted partner may have been holding her hand throughout the ordeal, his eyes were glued to the television as Manchester United played Juventus in the Champions League semi-final. There were more sighs and screams coming from me than there were from the labour ward as my team qualified for the final, which we won, but once Aaryn (or, for a brief period Alex Ryan Scholesy Campbell) arrived I felt that I finally had my own team to manage.

1999 had been a good year and now, as the new millennium dawned, my mind focused on Sydney and the Olympic Games. If UK officialdom had got its way, I would not have even been running the 200m in Sydney. The AAA Championships were held at Alexander Stadium, Birmingham, in July, where I finished second in the 100m in a time of 10.12 (only 0.01 of a second behind the champion Dwain Chambers), and won the 200m ahead of my good friend and training partner Christian Malcolm. These championships were, as they are now, the de-facto UK trials for the Olympic Games and I was arguably the most in-form sprinter in the country at the time. I was also a newly-crowned sprint relay world silver medallist. Yet, despite this, in the stadium car park after the trials I was approached by a UK Athletics official and told of the decision that I was only going to compete in the 100m and the sprint relay in Sydney. Someone, somewhere had decided that I was not going to run in the 200m.

The decision was not transparent and, considering that I was UK champion, not objective or justifiable. To have an official of UK Athletics – in this case a figure who was only significant in elite sport in so much as he wore a UK Athletics polo shirt now and again – break the news to me in a car park was disgraceful. The whole scenario was a sham and smacked of amateurism in the extreme. To say I lost my cool is an understatement. I let this official know exactly what I thought of the decision, his means of transmitting it and, for good measure, what I thought of him. I stated my case very aggressively and he quickly realised that I would hold him personally responsible – in a very public way – should I not be allowed to compete in the event I had won literally minutes earlier. Was I unprofessional in my outburst? Absolutely. Was he unprofessional and unaccountable in his decision and manner? Absolutely. The end result? I was on my way to Sydney, competing in both sprint events and the relay.

I had learned harsh but valuable lessons in Atlanta that would serve me well in these, my second Olympic Games. I took a much more serious approach and committed myself wholeheartedly: yes I'd savour the atmosphere and the spectacle, but I was only there to compete. The Olympic Games had played an important part in my life and the 1984 Los Angeles Games were the reason I was inspired to take up athletics in the first place. Being there in 1996 had been a fantastic experience, but I now realised that I needed to make my mark and create my own piece of sporting history.

There were other profoundly inspirational reasons for the Olympics being important for me. One was Luz Long's significant-yet-forgotten public gesture of friendship and solidarity toward Jesse Owens at the Berlin Olympics in 1936. Another was at the 1968 Games when the American athletes, Tommie Smith and John Carlos, held their black-gloved hands in the air during the 200m medal ceremony – thereafter named the 'black power' salute despite Smith stating that it was a human rights-related gesture – which is engrained in the political history of track and field.

Peter Norman, the Australian sprinter who finished in the silver medal position, wore an Olympic Project for Human Rights (OPHR) badge for the medal ceremony in solidarity with his fellow athletes, so all three – Tommie, John and Peter – sent out a powerful message to the world that day. Through their actions they made millions of people worldwide aware that there was something amiss and that change was needed. Their non-verbal protest against racism and poverty has stood the test of time to the extent that the silhouette of the three of them on the podium is as recognizable as the soldiers raising the US flag on Iwo Jima or the image of Che Guevara's face. We view Tommie Smith's action through the lens of history, yet as much as we can feel empowered, enabled or believe that we are as equal as we have ever been, the truth is rather more uncomfortable. The treatment of the NFL star Colin Kaepernick in 2017 proved this. His decision to kneel during the American anthem, in protest against the same abuses of human rights as Tommie Smith did in Mexico City, proved that little has changed in half a century. The fact that Kaepernick felt the need to make such a statement in 'the land of the free', shames western society.

I was lucky enough to meet Tommie Smith a couple of years after the Sydney Games and was very honoured to do so. Smith was a driving force and a revered figure to me as a black man, but also a trailblazer as a black athlete. He used his platform as a successful athlete to inspire others, and shone the antiseptic of daylight onto a dark wound within western culture – racism. I was a two-time Olympic medallist by the time I met him, but I wasn't sure he would know who I was. When the opportunity came I approached him as a respectful fan. He was a perfect gentleman and indulged my inquisitive nature. I could have spent hours in his company, talking about non-track issues as much as asking for pointers on becoming a better sprinter, yet I was not talking to him as a fellow sprinter – he was a cultural icon – and at the Sydney Games in 2000 I was fortunate enough to witness first-hand another truly historical cultural moment.

Cathy Freeman was the face of the Sydney Olympics in 2000. Her image was plastered everywhere, and the travelling media salivated at any opportunity to catch a glimpse of, or to interact with, her. She was an athlete who represented herself as a strong competitor, but she also represented Australia at an Australian Olympics. More significantly, she represented her Aboriginal heritage. An Aboriginal presence at the top table of an Olympic Games in Sydney would guarantee that the world's media would, at the very least, bring Australia's historically poor treatment of its indigenous people into the global conversation. To many oppressed peoples around the world she represented the persecuted becoming the celebrated.

Freeman, in her charming and gregarious way, exemplified the dignity of an indigenous nation; as an Aboriginal person she had as much reason as any to be bitter and hateful towards those who had for centuries, in the name of colonialism, subjugated and humiliated her people. Freeman's *own* grandmother was one of the so-called

'Stolen Generations', when Aboriginal children were forcibly removed from their parents and resettled with white families: a disgraceful and fundamentally racist Australian Government policy that lasted from 1910 until the 1970s. Freeman became a symbol of the potential for forgiveness, reconciliation and future harmony within Australia. This was politically significant, for only six years previously her gesture of carrying both the Australian and Aboriginal flags after her race at the 1994 Commonwealth Games in Victoria, Canada, led to her being appallingly reprimanded by her own Australian Commonwealth Association. Those six years between the Commonwealth and Olympic Games, however, evidently became time enough to change attitudes towards Aboriginal symbolism in Australia. In Sydney she was chosen as the (perfect) candidate for the highest honour in any Olympiad – lighting the flame. Freeman became the face of Australia, the face of the Games.

Away from all the symbolism of her presence, she was also the proclaimed favourite for the gold, and was anointed champion by her country folk even before stepping onto the track. There was, however, the small matter of delivering the gold medal in front of 112,000 expectant supporters who were packed into the Olympic Stadium for the women's 400m final. That level of pressure must have been immense. On the track she was competing against Marie-José Pérec (who ultimately withdrew), Lorraine Graham and Katharine Merry, but off the track she was competing against a subtext of enormous political and cultural significance. She needed to perform at these Games, not only for herself, but for her nation and for her people – both of whom, over the course of Australia's 20th century history, had been two different entities. For Cathy Freeman, winning at the 2000 Games wasn't just an opportunity to shine at sport, as it was for every other athlete at those Games. For her, and for Australia, it was an absolute necessity. A woman running a lap of a track faster than her competitors was to be the catalyst for healing deep wounds.

It is hard to imagine the weight that she carried for those 49 seconds, and when she eventually pulled away from the fast-finishing Graham and Merry to cross the line in first place, there was no feeling of exhilaration, it more a case of simple relief that the ordeal was over. Freeman exhibited superior mental strength to carry her through that whole experience. She would have been under no illusion as to what a missed opportunity for greatness it would have been had she not won gold. As a fellow athlete I considered myself blessed and honoured to have been in a position to share those moments with her. I was also delighted for Katharine Merry when she won the bronze, but this was double-edged for me because if Katharine had returned from Sydney as the only medallist from our training group, we would never have heard the last of it. Katharine, in this respect, became another inspiration for me.

There was also a fear, ingrained deeply within my own psyche, that since Atlanta I had trained exceptionally hard but that even if I gave it my all in Sydney, it would not be good enough. There were logistical distractions, in so much that Linford was not allowed to be anywhere near the facilities as he was technically a *persona non grata* with UK Athletics, and I had decided to stay outside the Olympic village because as an easily distracted person I didn't think it would be the best place for me to be successful.

Linford was coaching Katharine Merry and me, two genuine medal prospects. He had a real talent for demanding the best of me and I believe he had an understanding of what buttons to press, and at what times. The fact he could not be by my side the entire time was an unnecessary irritation. I had gone to Sydney to win and I had, as a part of my team, an individual who had taken on the world and won, yet now had to be kept at arm's length. Compared to the situation just a decade later, when UK Athletics seemingly had no qualms in embracing Alberto Salazar, the lack of consistency in decision-making was stark.

Despite the potential distractions and barriers I knew would be there, Sydney was a time when I had to be focused and the Games became a personal triumph for the little boy from Ashton-on-Mersey. I managed to experience the thrill of an Olympic individual sprint final not once, but twice.

I had run well in the 100m qualifying rounds and got through to the final with an outside chance of a medal. Being on the start line for an Olympic final is probably the same as walking out on Centre Court for a Wimbledon final, or taking the field at Lord's for a Test match, yet being under starter's orders for an Olympic sprint final is a strange experience. The concentration on the task ahead overrides everything. In almost every life-changing sporting experience, from running out at Soldier Field, Chicago, or standing in front of 80,000 people at

Twickenham, you get to savour the moment. You are aware that your entire life's sacrifices have led you to this point, but no enjoyment or awareness of its significance is allowed to marinade your soul.

The fact that the entire experience on the track – from leaving the tunnel, to returning down the tunnel – lasts maybe ten minutes, robs you of savouring your time on the grand stage. Having spoken to top-level performers in other sports, the taste of the arena and the fizz of the experience – especially in team sports – lasts for over two hours; enough time to absorb every taste and sound. Being on the blocks, however, completely surrounded by such a deathly hush, stimulated my mind to take me to all kinds of unnecessary places. Those final few seconds before the starter's gun fired was a scenario I had dreamt of for over 20 years, and here I was, on the starting blocks in an Olympic final. At that very moment it dawned on me where I was, I lost my focus and the nerves engulfed me.

In the 100m final I was drawn in lane one. Despite exploding out of the blocks more powerfully than I had ever done before, under the flickering flashbulbs of the Sydney sky I saw my attempt at a medal in the blue riband event disappear after about 50 metres. At that point I was in contention with the race leaders, but then Maurice Greene and Ato Boldon put on their respective afterburners and ran away from the field. I finished a creditable 6th, but Greene's 9.88 seconds performance was insurmountable. I gained confidence from this performance, however, and felt that my speed and power could place me in a strong position for my 200m campaign.

I had learned from Colin Jackson, years earlier, about the value of strategising a race. His level of detail and preparation was meticulous. Prior to my assault on the 200m in Sydney, I had decided to adopt a similar approach, and concentrate a significant amount of work on one aspect of the race that I was not known for: running the bend. My thoughts were based around 'surprising my competitors' that a prior weakness could become a strength.

As competitive athletes, we all had an idea as to who excelled during specific parts of a race, and there was an element of opposition analysis, and opposition awareness. Some, such as Ato Boldon, were awesome at the start while others, like Asafa Powell, came through with strength, mid-race. I was relatively uniform throughout most races but in the 200m a strong aggressive bend could propel me ahead. This aspect of my running needed specific attention so Colin Jackson's former training partner, and now both retired athlete and international rugby player, Nigel Walker, helped me enormously in this regard. With Nigel I practised and refined the art of bend running.

As a skill, the very nature of running a bend depended on upon some level of imbalance. Unlike a NASCAR on the Indianapolis 500 track, bend running wasn't just quite as simple as putting the pedal to the metal and holding an almost continuous left turn. Nigel would, in time, become the head of the English Institute of Sport, and his intelligence and analytical nature gave me a significant advantage during this time. We figured that by breaking up the bend into sections, and applying every detail of my sprinting – my running gait, my height and my acceleration – to each of these sections, I could negotiate the bend and at the same time shave hundredths of a second off my time as I exploded into the straight. Doing this also focused my mind to bring something new to my armoury as a sprinter. Instead of simply preparing to be as powerful and as fast as I could be, I was also analysing the event's demands – from the finish line backwards. My maturity as an athlete and as a person was now leading me to make better choices for my preparation. I hoped these would pay off in the 200m final.

I had made a positive decision to stay away from the distractions of the Olympic village as much as possible during the Sydney Games, but before the 200m I ventured in to catch up with a few of my fellow athletes. Part of the mystical power of the Olympic Games is that it helps competitors to cultivate life-long friendships with teammates in other sports, and with athletes from other countries. During my visit I bumped into boxer Audley Harrison who had captivated the British public with his fantastic displays of power and precision in reaching the super-heavyweight boxing final. Audley had already won a silver medal, but had frustratingly broken his hand in the process of progressing to the final. This didn't matter, though. He was going to fight on. He was a true warrior. I was so inspired that he was willing to fight in the final with only one 'good' hand in order to fulfil his dream of being Olympic champion, which he did. He never gave up. His attitude elevated my own thinking and provided an additional jolt of energy and determination before my 200m final. Our friendship grew after the Games and a year later I was deeply honoured to be invited as a guest to Audley and Raychel's wedding in Jamaica.

There was a wealth of quality in this Olympic final, including Ato Boldon – who had won a silver medal in the 100m a few days earlier – as well as the favourite for the event, John Capel, from the USA. Capel had run some superfast times in the lead-up to Sydney and, based on form, was the bookmakers' choice to win. Unknown to me at the time, however, this was when a little-known Greek 400m runner from the Budapest 1998 European Championships semi-finals would come to play a huge part in my story. In true Shakespearian fashion, covertly yet significantly, he appeared well into the third act. I was drawn in lane 6, and one lane inside me was Konstantinos Kenteris.

It was 28 September 2000 and, back in Manchester, my mother and my sister had been joined in their living room by many of the UK media. Having performed so well in the qualifying rounds, there was a distinct feeling that there might be an Olympic gold medal heading to Sale Racecourse. The *Manchester Evening News*, BBC Northwest and a few local radio stations had sent their cameras, microphones and reporters to capture the occasion as Marva and Sophia Campbell watched in anticipation of me achieving the unthinkable.

I tore out of the blocks and ran the best bend of my entire life. John Capel started poorly, having flinched and almost false-started, whereas I was already up on Ato Boldon as we reached mid-bend. The hours and days spent with Nigel Walker had paid huge dividends, and as we hit the top of the bend and entered the home straight I was probably half a metre ahead of the rest of the field. Marva shot up and put her hands to her mouth as she saw 'her Darren' lead in the Olympic final and make the turn into the home straight in pole position. Sophia's heart was in her mouth, every muscle in her body tensed, as she braced to explode into utter euphoria while counting down the seconds to her brother crossing the line and winning Olympic gold. Both mother and daughter had viewed the 200m as an afterthought, thinking the Olympics were over for me as soon as I had finished 6th in the 100m. Now they stood in the living room of Marva's Sale home, their nerves stretched to the limit as they willed me on to stay ahead for just long enough to cross the line ahead of the rest.

Coming off the bend, the athletes in the outside lanes were comfortably ahead of the rest, and it seemed the medals were going to

Manchester; Barbados (Obadele Thompson, lane 7) and Trinidad and Tobago (Ato Boldon, lane 8). Everyone else including Capel, Kenteris and Christian Malcolm were surely too far behind.

With 50m to go, I ran past the podium where the medals would be presented believing the ambition I had nurtured since that fateful day, when I returned to school at Ashton-on-Mersey and got mocked for having unrealistic pipedreams, was about to be realised. Yet no-one had accounted for Kenteris. None of the athletes. No commentators. No mother. No sister. Like a racehorse that had been held back until the final furlong, a blue and white streak tore past in seventh gear. He crossed the line, arms aloft like a modern day Achilles, and despite my fast-finishing lunge I was half a stride behind him at the crucial time. Konstantinos Kenteris became the surprise Olympic champion.

Surprise is probably an understatement. Nobody saw it coming. I for one certainly didn't see it coming and I was in the lane next to him with 30 metres to go. His timeline to gold was, performance-wise, in a word, astonishing. A few days before I won the 100m gold at the 1998 European Championships in Budapest, Kenteris had bowed out of the 400m in the semi-finals. His 200m personal best at that time was a modest 20.83 seconds, which placed him outside of the top *four thousand* all-time best performances recorded for the distance. Whatever happened in the intervening two years to make him Olympic champion in a time of 20.09 was absolutely phenomenal. His 100m had gone from a social-athlete level time of 10.52 seconds in 1999 to an international standard 10.16 seconds merely 12 months later. Kenteris had improved almost ten metres in a year. It brought me no solace that it was in those final ten metres of the 200m that I had gone from gold to silver, with the blue and white colours of Greece striding past on my inside.

Many of my fellow athletes, from all nations, whispered their thoughts on how such performances had been achieved. I was overjoyed with my silver and bore no bitterness or anger whatsoever at whomever took the top spot on the podium. I thought it might have been Capel, Boldon, or myself, but I looked at my silver with immense pride. My peers however were not so gracious, and threw all kinds of innuendos into the conversation regarding the colour of the medal I had won, or maybe should have won. I knew at the time such comments were made with a sense of solidarity but they were also tinged with cruelty.

They were unintentionally belittling my phenomenal achievement of Olympic silver and also there was a sense of heartlessness in making me hope that I would possibly get gold. Also, such comments obviously belittled Kenteris' fantastic achievement of winning Olympic gold.

It affected me to the extent that I woke up on the morning of 29 September not with a beaming smile that befitted an Olympic silver medallist, but to the echo of a fellow competitor's words ringing in my ears: "Don't worry, by the morning your silver will be gold".

It got to the point that I was told to half expect a knock on the door or a phone call to confirm what a lot of athletes were thinking. The prospect of being promoted to Olympic gold was the talk of the entire team, and it certainly consumed my mind. Teammates were constantly asking me, "Have you heard anything yet?" and there an unspoken understanding in the Olympic village that there was a high chance that Kenteris' gold would be subject to further scrutiny. I felt like spelling out to my teammates – wait a second, I've just won Olympic silver here. Forget about him – give me some respect.

Yet, as history now tells us, four years on from Sydney the innuendos went thermonuclear. Kenteris and Thanou, the Greek sprinters carrying the hopes of the entire nation, had now been hospitalised and withdrawn from the Athens Olympics on the eve of the Games 'in the interests of the country'. Confusion reigned supreme. Had they missed drug tests prior to the Games? Had they really been involved in a motorcycle accident or was the whole thing concocted as an alibi? At first, the Greek judicial system found them both guilty of perjury over the motorcycle crash scandal – which could have encouraged the athletics world to re-examine the veracity of their track performances – but then acquitted them both on appeal due to 'reasonable doubt'. There was no proof to confirm the truth or dispel the lie concerning the crash.

The court did uphold the conviction of their coach for the storage of illegal substances but suspended his sentence. Later, in June 2006, both athletes reached an out-of-court settlement with the IAAF for anti-doping rule violations, accepting that they had missed tests between July and August 2004, prior to the Athens Games. The official record states, to this day, that there were no failed drug tests by either Thanou or Kenteris, and it really doesn't take off the sheen from the Olympic silver that I have proudly kept at home. To be honest, at the time, I was not completely stupid either. I wasn't going to kick up a fuss in Sydney in the knowledge that the next Olympics were in Greece, and that I was effectively going to be gunning for the hero of the Athens Olympics. That would have been career suicide. I look back at my Sydney performance with as much pride as anything else from my career. I treasure the silver medal and the only bitterness I feel is that the controversy slightly detracted from my own achievement.

The penultimate event on the track is, historically, the 4 x 100m and in Sydney we genuinely believed our team was in a strong position to win considering the previous year's silver medal in Seville, but we were also wiser and more humble having learned from the harrowing mistake of four years earlier. The component parts of the quartet were as close to a British sprint dream-team for the new millennium as you could hope to get.

Jason Gardener was a sub-10 second 100m runner, and his nickname of the Bath Bullet wasn't only deserved but consistently proven correct. In an event like a relay, where getting in front can place huge pressure on others due to the stagger effect of the bends, Jason wasn't just a team member, he was a weapon. Christian Malcolm had finished fifth in the 200m final and was at the peak of his outstanding career. Christian was one of the most naturally talented and elegant athletes to have ever put on the GB vest and his speed and grace while in full flight were a source of inspiration for us as a team. If we could get the baton to him early, this laid-back wisecracker from Newport wouldn't have let anything affect his performance. He was a real asset to our quartet.

Having Dwain Chambers on the team was a massively destabilising factor for our competitors. He had finished fourth, and agonisingly close to the medals, in the 100m event, but more than just his raw speed, his physical presence alone was intimidating. Furthermore, he trained with a number of the Americans and having him in such close proximity would be unsettling for them in the final moments prior to the event. He had an authority and air about him on the track that I hadn't seen since Linford Christie - they certainly knew he was there. I had a gleaming silver medal around my neck from the 200m, and having also finished sixth in the 100m my confidence in my own ability, and also in my team's prowess, was sky high. The cards were decked favourably for us.

The 4 x 100m relay heats were on the day after my 200m final, so I didn't take part. Unfortunately I had the torturous privilege of watching a disaster unfold as Jason and Allyn Condon, like me in the previous Olympics, weren't synchronised enough in the changeover and vital milliseconds were lost. Marlon and Dwain then completely mis-timed their changeover, and Dwain assumed my role at the Atlanta Olympics of being the one to scream skywards at the agony of it all while failing to carry the baton to the finishing line – a second howler in as many Olympics. We had the components to succeed, we had the talent, and we certainly had the confidence. However, I realised yet again that confidence counts for nothing when you can't execute. Inside I was screaming. As a quartet, we had another reason to eat humble pie, and we would all have to wait another full Olympic four-year cycle to make amends.

My first Olympics in Atlanta made me feel like an athlete. My second in Sydney validated my dream of being a winner. The wind had filled my sails after the Olympic Games, and after winning the 100m Grand Prix final in Doha a week after Sydney I wished the season still had months to run. The victory in Doha was not only a prestigious race to win, it was also a very lucrative event which enabled me to pocket a deposit for a house I had seen in Rogerstone, just outside Newport. Owning my own home had always been an aspiration for me, as it was for many people with my background, and my personal life was falling into shape. I had achieved a huge part of my athletic ambitions, and I had a wonderful partner in Clair and baby son Aaryn, waiting at home to share in my triumph. Life could not have been better.

This was so very apparent when I returned to a hero's welcome among my family and friends at Sale. I travelled up to Manchester with my medal and a smile as wide as the M6. As soon as I indicated to turn into the Racecourse Estate a bout of self-awareness hit me like a hammer. What would my younger self think of this flash idiot turning up in his brand new Jaguar XK8 and flashing his Olympic sliver bling. 'Dick head' – that's what I thought to myself – 'I can't bring this car on to the estate. I'm not thinking straight. I need to be normal Sale Racecourse Darren'.

I called Lynx. He laughed, but totally understood my predicament. He knew my intentions were good in coming back but also realised how it would look. He immediately brought me crashing down to earth with some sense: "Nobody around here is going to believe that you have an Olympic medal. People from here need to see things that can be gotten with a dream and some hard work ... and they won't believe it until they see it."

Holding the medal in the Olympic village after the race brought me such personal joy, but seeing my friends hold it in our house in Sale Racecourse – 'proud' doesn't do it justice. It was an achievement for us all. People on this estate often obtained things by dubious means, but the medal that they held in their hands that day – the one that they had seen on television – had been achieved in the right way. I felt pride in conveying that message.

Things aren't hyped for the sake of it by the people in Moss Side or Sale Racecourse, so when I sat down with Lynx and Mum in the house later that night, I asked about how they felt. They both laughed and said that they always knew I was always going to overachieve. It felt as if they'd believed it would be a foregone conclusion, or preordained. It also made me feel grounded. It made me feel that they weren't going to be that impressed until I returned with a gold medal.

Bloody hard to please, some people.

8

Manchester

"Do it for Manchester, Darren!"

I was eager to use Sydney as a springboard to greater things and although I basked in the warm glow of Olympic silver, it was not enough. My dream had always been to stand on the top of the podium. I had always wanted to be an Olympic gold medallist. To come so tantalisingly close was a huge confidence boost, but also a reminder that I had to keep working for four more years to have a chance of fulfilling a life's dream. Holding an Olympic medal in my hand while sitting on the sofa at home brought a degree of satisfaction, but it only lasted to a point. The fire for gold was still burning inside me. That meant four more years of slog. Sydney 2000 had been a test of my physical abilities. The next 18 months were a test of my emotional and psychological faculties.

I began the 2001 season in Austin, Texas, following a block of training in the American sun. I ran 10.16 seconds for the 100m – one of the quickest openings to a season I had ever achieved – but that would be it for me in 2001. My hamstring started limiting my training and one frustration soon led to another until one day it gave in completely. It was torn at the insertion. To suffer such a serious injury at the start of the season was a huge blow and, to make matter worse, things were not going well at home, either. A downward spiral of domestic unhappiness affected my athletics which then, in turn, caused more tension at home. My fiery nature, when faced with adversity, didn't help the situation. From my days at Sale Racecourse,

I had learned to control what I could, and steer clear of things that I couldn't. To find myself unable to exert a positive, guiding influence over the things that mattered most in my life – my family and sporting career – was new territory.

Being a good dad had always been a personal priority as well as a parental duty. To be able to carry out this role in the way that I wanted, especially since I had been deprived of it myself, I felt an inherent need to be the provider, the role model, the man of the house. The fact that these were linked to my success as an athlete drove me to realise that both aspects were not only aligned but dependent on one another. I was unable to focus on my athletics career unless I felt that I was fulfilling the role of being a strong father and provider, and I was limited in my capacity to do that without the financial and emotional strength of succeeding at my job.

When my core foundations – as father and provider – began to crumble, so did I. Low on confidence, I became frustrated, short-tempered and hard to live with. The fragility of my own self-esteem became horribly exposed when I failed to cope and I went through a period of significant self-doubt as a father. I had no reference points for what it took to be a good father. My intentions, however, were sincere and genuine. As an athlete, I knew I was getting older and realised that there might be more good days behind me than ahead.

I believe I was suffering from post-career depression in the middle of my career. I was injured, unable to showcase my talent, unable to provide for my family in the way that I wanted, and completely unable to exude warmth and love. Aaryn was three, and Clair was experiencing the emotions and demands that any new mother goes through. I was there yet absent at the same time. It was a challenging and horrible time for both of us. I didn't want to do anything, and I was not a particularly nice guy to be around.

Before long, it all got too much – for both of us – so I took some time out to figure out where we were as a family and as a couple. The trauma of opening up, being honest about mental health issues, not hiding behind the persona of an alpha male wasn't something that was discussed in the early 2000s. Two decades down the line sport would be at the forefront of this struggle but there was no way a Moss Side boy, now at the height of his career, was going to admit to having any such issues.

Consequently, by talking to the media while struggling with my mental health, when the darkest of dark thoughts had embedded themselves my head, I paid a very hefty price, and in a few interviews with newspapers that year the sensational story of the athlete Darren Campbell being on the brink of the unthinkable was printed, including a front-page headline in the *Manchester Evening News*: 'Darren: I was on the Brink of Suicide'. It wasn't quite as clear cut as that but, as many others who have struggled with depression will understand, I contemplated every possible option to lessen the pain for myself and for my family.

While in the deep pit of negative thoughts, options I'd never previous contemplated began to look like perfect sense. I felt that my negativity was toxic for those around me, and that it would actually benefit them if I simply wasn't around anymore. When you are in that frame of mind, removing an unpredictable poisonous constant from their lives seems totally logical and the most caring thing you can do for those you love. I wasn't necessarily considering ending my own life, it was more a case of just removing myself from their lives by moving away and enabling them to carry on without having to shoulder the extra weight of 'me'. However, it soon struck me that, by taking that course of action, the sins of the father would be passed on to the son. It would have placed Aaryn in the same situation that I had been in 26 years earlier, yet in this depressive state it was exactly what I was contemplating.

I felt I had no career, no family and no reason to smile. Being away from my son on my birthday was utterly soul destroying. That year, my birthday was the day after the terrorist attack on the World Trade Centre's twin towers in New York. This was an event which sent tidal waves of horror and fear around the globe, and as I sat alone on my sofa in an increasing state of despair and self-pity. It seemed that the world itself was on fire and descending to an unfathomably bad place.

In these circumstances, to halt the fall into darkness, having a potentially joyful occasion or important event to look forward to can be invaluable. What was my saving grace? The Commonwealth Games in Manchester. Had they been anywhere else in the world I doubt I would have been so focused, or my quest for personal redemption so great, but the Commonwealth Games being held in Manchester played a part in getting me back on track, personally and professionally. My home city was staging a major championships and it was an opportunity too good to miss.

Nathan Blake reached out to me and I went to stay with him to try and get my head back on track. I just needed someone to talk to and he was a great listener. He made me realise the importance of sharing problems with a trusted friend, and was a huge help for me during this time.

I felt that I had travelled the world and represented myself as an athlete, as a patriotic Englishman of Jamaican heritage, and a British sportsman, but having lived in Wales for so long I now realised that I had not tipped my hat, in a professional capacity, to my home city. Linford was a proud Londoner, Colin was Cardiff through and through, and I was proud of my roots but I had not shouted this from any rooftops. I had seen the responsibility, and the boost, that the Olympics being in Sydney had given Cathy Freeman and despite the fact that the Commonwealths were perceived by some as a less important international sporting competition, in an athletics sense, it still featured most of the powerhouses of world sprinting outside of the USA. One could argue, for sprinting in particular, that it was more difficult to win a medal at the Commonwealths than at many other international championships. The prospect of not just representing England, but also Manchester – *in Manchester* – was tantalising. Yet, to an injured, depressed athlete separated from his family and going through a mid-career crisis, these traits were not ideal for my preparation, to say the least.

With Ato Bolden, Obadele Thompson, Christian Malcolm and me all due to compete, four of the first five finishers at the Sydney 200m final were going to be at the Commonwealth Games. If that wasn't a strong enough field, knowing that Asafa Powell, Frankie Fredericks, Kim Collins, Dwain Chambers and Marlon Devonish would also be there, I began to worry if I would even make the final. The polarised thoughts of being inspired, yet at the same time petrified, by a 'hometown' Commonwealth Games added to my unbalanced mindset.

The week between Christmas and New Year in 2001 became a pivotal time in my life. I was living alone – having separated from Clair – and on Christmas Day I experienced a life-changing moment. On Christmas morning, I became just another father visiting his child and watch him opening his presents. This was an all-too-common scenario the world over and one which I had never considered would cross my path. Every absent father has his own reason for being away from home on important occasions and I began to understand this during the period when Clair and I were separated. What I didn't comprehend, though, until I experienced it myself, was the heavyweight punch to the heart that the act of leaving your child on Christmas Day felt like. It hurt. It really hurt.

Having given Aaryn his presents I left the house in tears, my mind replaying the comments and criticism I knew would be said if I revealed my self-pity: "If you were home you wouldn't have to leave in the first place." Nathan Blake and his mother, Yvonne, had very kindly invited me to have Christmas Dinner with them, and I arrived feeling absolutely broken. I wasn't exactly bringing tidings of great joy to their festive home. While we were having our Christmas dinner, Nathan's mum asked me a very simple question but it was one which shook me to my very core: "I can tell that you are a serious guy, but you are always joking around – why are you always joking?"

She was clearly a very clever woman and had identified humour as my psychological coping mechanism. My low confidence and lower ebb was masked – as it often is – with jovial behaviour. I couldn't give her a credible answer. In a sense, it was probably a rhetorical question, but it was the right one because it made me think. She had been a good friend to me that day, and it was with a sense of great pride that, a few years later, I presented her with the winner's bouquet of flowers from a Diamond League meeting as a 'Thank You'. Yvonne is sadly no longer with us, but I never forgot her timely, pointed but well meant intervention.

The light that helped guide me towards my hometown Commonwealth Games shone, of all places, from a mountainside village called Llanwynno between the Rhondda and Cynon valleys, and involved a half-true/half-mythical story about a legendary runner. I was approached by the organisers of the Nos Galan race in Mountain Ash, and asked to be their 'mystery runner' for the 2001 event. The Nos Galan (New Year's Eve) race was a celebration of the life and exploits of the legendary 18th century Welsh runner Guto Nyth Brân. Being asked to be the 'mystery runner' was an honour reserved for sporting celebrities who, in the past, had included Mary Rand and David Hemery. My initial feelings upon being asked to do this was a mixture of pride, on one hand, and serious reservations on the other.

MANCHESTER

I had been exceptionally low for the preceding six to nine months, and the prospect of representing myself as an athlete at an event that had thousands of people lining the streets wasn't an attractive one. We all like to present an image to others of happiness, vitality and strength, but being devoid of all three, due to my personal turmoil, meant being in the public eye even for one night sounded like a very bad idea. Also, with the event being a 5km race I thought there would be no way I would run further than 400m: the disconnect between the perception of me being an Olympic medallist and the reality of a weary body languishing towards the end of an endurance run would be painful to see. However, I desperately needed to make proactive decisions that would reverse the negative cycle that I had found myself in.

I agreed to the request but remained unsure if I could do it. I wasn't regarded as an unreliable person, but I had fallen into a chasm of depressive behaviour and I wanted to hedge my bets and see how I would feel in the days leading up to the race. On the night itself, I dragged myself out of the house, partly due to a sense of duty – I couldn't let the organisers and participants down – and partly to take my mind off how rubbish my life had become, for at least one night.

In Mountain Ash I learnt that we can all find inspiration from the most unlikely of places. The Sydney Olympic silver medallist found his in a mass participation 5k race in the middle of the night on a cold mountainside village in Wales. My positive mindset started to come back simply from being there. Seeing hundreds of runners braving the weather with smiles on their faces while standing patiently in the cold and wind as dignitaries made their speeches and introduced guests made me feel embarrassed. They were excited to run alongside me and share their own stories and experiences, whereas I had been viewing life as a negative dark chore.

Many people would suggest warm weather and cocktails in the sun as antidotes for feeling gloomy. I was in Mountain Ash, at midnight, in the middle of winter. Even the name of the place sounded like somewhere rugged and dark contrived by JRR Tolkien where you expected to see a fork-tongued dragon. This could not be further from the truth. I found salvation and fun amongst hardly souls whose frozen toes and tired limbs managed to drag themselves around the town at 1am. Their contagious smiles, humour and 'What on earth are we doing here? We should be at home downing some Penderyn whisky and watching Jools Holland on the box' attitude re-ignited within me the flame of positivity and, dare I say it, a smile and some laughter. For the first time in months, I felt energised.

Another unexpected intervention came, again, from Nathan Blake. Kevin Williams, his friend, was training for the Commonwealth Games, where he'd represent Wales, and part of his training schedule involved scaling the sand dunes around Merthyr Mawr near Bridgend. It was here that Nathan used to work on his endurance prior to the football season, and now he was sharing his knowledge and experience with both his friend and me. The irony in all of this was that Kevin and I were not only housemates, but would also be prospective competitors in the upcoming Commonwealths. I knew Wales was a small country but this was ridiculous! As an 'introduction' to the dunes, Nathan took me on a route from the car park, climbing several peaks, squeezing through hedges, side-stepping rabbit holes and goodness knows what else until we reached the sea. By the time we had completed the circuit I swear I could see six moons in the sky.

I knew from my limited time as a footballer that their training methods had helped me with my endurance – Budapest had confirmed this, but training with Nathan proved hugely beneficial on both the physical and mental levels. It was fun, it was exhilarating and we built up a real sense of camaraderie. I became the beneficiary of exercise-induced healing. This might sound strange for an athlete to state the benefits of running, but this was completely different from what I had done before and I was now in a completely different state of mind. I had hit rock-bottom, the Nos Galan race had illuminated the path out of my darkness and I was now climbing out of it with the help of sand, sheer exhaustion, and lots of post-session hugs and smiles. I realised that depression had left me in a state where I was constantly operating at a heightened state of anxiety. Whereas previously in my life the stress created by an argument or disagreement was a mere ripple in the shallow end, it had now taken a firmer grip on me and was now generating waves that could engulf me, if I didn't grasp the problem.

What became a litmus test for my recovery, both as an athlete and as a person, were the 2002 Commonwealth Games trials – the first event to be held in the new City of Manchester Stadium. I had a heavy cold and was coughing and spluttering – Jamie Baulch had been trying to get me to lay low for a day or so in order to recuperate as he could see I was ill – but despite knowing full well that this would never be accepted as an excuse I managed to drag myself to fourth in the 100m. I was so desperate to be selected for the Games I asked Linford and his coach Ron Rodden if there was anything technically problematic in my running that could cause such under-performance. For them both to come up blank should have given me encouragement that I was performing well. I should have realised that having a heavy cold would sap my energy somewhat. Ultimately, a doctor prescribed medication for what was a seriously badly-timed virus. The trials became a frustrating disappointment.

The gap between the 'top five' in the England team – Dwain Chambers, Mark Lewis-Francis, Marlon Devonish, Jason Gardener and me – was wafer-thin, and Chris Lambert was also closing in fast. It would be disrespectful to any of these athletes to suggest they didn't merit selection to the Games and yet, remarkably, that is precisely what I was subjected to. I suffered a certain amount of criticism from a few peers – including John Regis – who articulated the view held by some that I hadn't proved myself as being in any form and should not be selected. John was, of course, entitled to his opinion as much as the next commentator, but those who have been in the competitive arena know the fluctuations that occur in performance, and as a result of injury in the preparation for major championships. I took this criticism a little to heart because it was relatively unwarranted. Had I not been picked, I would have been disappointed, of course, but I would've been aware of the wider context and the high standard that lay within the England team at the time.

I would have accepted the decision in the full knowledge that because of this great strength in depth, only a few could be selected, and that the trials had to play a part in the selection process. I was, however, the reigning Olympic silver medallist for that same distance. Fortunately, my name was included on the list for the Manchester Games and I could breathe a sigh of relief, and focus on the preparation in the limited time I had left.

As my career progressed, I found myself becoming more and more interested in the intricacies of the sport. I was becoming a 'student of the game'. I realised that across many sports, the better managers and players – from Sir Alex Ferguson and Thierry Henry in football, to

Phil Jackson and Michael Jordan in basketball – prided themselves in bringing an analytical and scholarly approach to their preparation. This was before the age of GPS and sport science technologies, but adopting this strategic approach, aligned with my interest in chess, I strived to embrace this attitude.

Interestingly, at that time in British athletics there was a cohort of athletes who came together in a Bible group and who asked fellow athletes, such as Jonathan Edwards, for advice on training, programming and techniques. It became a regular occurrence. I used to try and pick the brains of the best and I asked the likes of Michael Johnson and Denise Lewis questions about their training to the extent where I felt like an undergraduate asking the advice of the professor. One of the best pieces of training advice that Tommie Smith had given me was to know my body better than anyone else, including my coach. He said: "Some days, if your coach asks for eight runs, do ten, because on other days he'll ask you for eight and you may only manage six."

I prepared according to the advice that Tommie had given me, and saw it as a way of controlling my destiny. So when I was selected for both the 200m and the relay, I summoned every ounce of competitive ruthlessness I had. With the virus subsiding, I managed to finish second in both sprint events in the AAA Championships and two weeks before the Commonwealths, my form was slowly returning but I wasn't as fluid as I should have been. The winter months had been spent more in a state of sadness at my family situation than creating a solid platform via conditioning work, and those things always catch up with you. You can't complain about the results you don't get from the work you haven't done.

Clair and I were slowly reconciling, so the light at the end of the tunnel was getting brighter. This was an enormous lift, for I had missed her and Aaryn terribly. I had my own professional motivation to succeed in Manchester, but there was now an element of repaying faith in those who had stuck by me in my personal life, which added an extra impetus. This was going to be a special championships for me, and by the eve of the Games, I was truly overwhelmed to have received so much warmth and encouragement from the city of Manchester. The officials, the fans, the Games staff, the volunteers, even the media, all gave me such love and support. The fact that my family were there for me also provided huge emotional inspiration.

MANCHESTER

To be given the honour of carrying the English flag at the opening ceremony in Manchester was a momentous milestone for the Campbell family, and 25 July 2002 is a date that will live long in the memory. Team England included sporting icons such as Jonathan Edwards, Kelly Holmes, Paula Radcliffe and Bradley Wiggins, so to be asked to lead my teammates into the stadium was truly humbling. It was only ten miles from Sale Racecourse to the City of Manchester Stadium, but they were a lifetime apart for a boy raised on the streets. It had been a 20-year journey during which I'd overcome deprivation, discrimination and depression, and now I was bestowed with the ultimate privilege in my home town for which I will always be thankful. I was overflowing with confidence, pride and vitality.

Four days later I would enter the same stadium tired, empty and frail. The rounds of the 200m had taken a significant toll on my body that was, in truth, unprepared and not ready for the rigours of an emotion-filled week, combined with the demands of elite sport. Manchester, as a city, had given me the energy and hunger to dig deep, but I was reaching the bottom of my reserves. As I walked to the blocks for the final, for which I'd qualified in eight place of eight, I could feel the roar of the crowd as thousands of Mancunians were loudly urging me on. At one point I heard a voice shouting encouragement to me: "Come on Darren you can do this. Do it for Manchester, Darren!"

I was so tired that my main concern was to not disappoint my teammates, my family, and my supporters by finishing last. I actually started to well up with emotion, such was the support of the crowd. They empowered me. I had been weak and was shaking, but during that walk to the blocks I started to believe, to comprehend that I could achieve over and above what I thought I was capable of.

I had no right to medal at that race: I wasn't fit enough, I hadn't been able to train well enough during the winter, and I was tired, but the occasion, and the crowd, lifted me and helped me to find an extra two or three gears. I was the slowest qualifier, but the crowd and the emotion carried me to a bronze medal behind Frankie Fredericks and Marlon Devonish. Sheer competitive spirit had forced me around the track in 20.2 seconds and, at that point in my career, the Commonwealth bronze equated to the best performance of my life. I was absolutely beside myself with joy. Medalling at a major championships, in my home town, having had the worst preparation

– personally and professionally – was beyond my wildest dreams. Only six months earlier I had been lying on the sofa, suffering from depression, and looking for an excuse to avoid a public appearance at a fun run in Wales. I had never been prouder of myself, and I knew all my family were in the crowd sharing my exhilaration.

We won gold in the relay, which was a fantastic feeling, but this paled in comparison with how I felt after the 200m. My inner doubts and demons were truly defeated in that race. I had proved to myself, for maybe the third or fourth time in my life, that despite overwhelming odds, determination could deliver success.

A week later the European Championships were held in Munich, and I was going there as the reigning European 100m champion. I was still riding the emotion and elation of Manchester but, crucially, having left early for Munich I had managed to sleep for a week and felt rested and much more relaxed. I also took the opportunity to link up with Dr Müller-Wohlfahrt who treated me in his clinic.

These championships were an opportunity to finish the season on a high, but they became more notorious for losing medals as much as winning them. Dwain Chambers won the 100m, blazing his way ahead of the rest of the field and crossing the line triumphantly in 9.96 seconds, ahead of Francis Obikwelu of Portugal and me in third place. Dwain was also a part of the victorious 4 x 100m relay team with whom I won gold. Both victories were to be annulled, however, because of Dwain's positive drug test results: a gold and a bronze were replaced by a silver. I was delighted for Francis in his winning the gold, as he was an athlete whom I hugely respected. He had previously been a footballer in Nigeria and given this up to become a Portuguese athlete, working briefly as a construction worker in the interim. Our journeys to the top of track and field had been very similar.

In the 200m I was disqualified in the heats for stepping out of my lane, but in truth this was academic because Konstantinos Kenteris, the Sydney Olympic champion, was in the process of cementing his personal dominance of the event. In the lead up to his home Olympic Games in Athens he had recorded a phenomenal 19.85 performance, finishing a full half second ahead of Francis and Marlon. Kenteris was as dominant in the 200m as Dwain had been in the 100m.

During the time I was laid up by injury, my personal and professional life had been a disaster. In the off-season I could easily have decided to jettison the forthcoming season and re-boot or not start back again at all. As it happened, the season proved that even in the most difficult of circumstances, I had this innate, ingrained stubbornness to want to compete and to succeed. As the song goes, my 'darkest hour was just before dawn'. Winning gold, silver and bronze in 2002 had to be regarded as a personal triumph.

Yet this rollercoaster calendar year still had an ace up its sleeve. At the end of the season, I heard whispers that Jason Gardener, one of my peers and competitors, had left his coach. Jason was a diminutive figure but exceptionally powerful and strong. Being svelte yet powerful ensured that he was quite possibly the most impressive sprint starter in the world. It was like having a Formula One engine in a BMW. His – now former – coach, Dave Lease, also lived in Wales, in fact just a few miles up the road from where I was based. This was a very convenient coincidence, so I decided to get in touch with him.

I mentioned to Dave that Jason's strength and his starting ability was something I coveted, and pleaded my case that I needed him to make me even better than Jason in those aspects. I hoped that in so doing I would gain his trust. This proved to be an inspired act, as Dave agreed and became a crucial part of the jigsaw. My thirst for further knowledge of the sport was met with an athletics intellectual who was equally as keen in sharing it. I learned about the different energy systems – alactic, anaerobic, and aerobic – and how you used them at specific points in training and in races, and how to maximise the results of using them all. I became his scientific project.

We worked on making my power-to-weight ratio as high as it could be. I lost a little weight but gained strength and power at the same time. He worked on my technique in the gym by incorporating traditional Olympic weightlifting and the latest digital technology. We used sophisticated biomechanical apparatus at Cardiff Metropolitan University to push my training analytics to levels I'd never previously experienced. This kind of performance analytic software was new to academia, and through Dave and the staff at the university I was truly at the cutting edge of such a sports science arms race.

Having previously learnt some valuable lessons from Colin Jackson, I decided to own every single aspect of my preparation. This included a little magic box that had been specifically built for our training group and which became something of an obsession. It was Linford's very own 'Start Machine Box', and consisted of a circuit box emitting two beeps, randomly sequenced apart, which simulated the two aspects of race starts: 'get set' and 'go'. Linford, Colin and Olympic hurdles champion Mark McCoy had used this nifty little contraption to their benefit previously and I got into the habit of using it every night by the side of my bed before going to sleep. Two beeps – over and over again – to practice the start position and my reactions. Simple things, but constantly reinforcing the little aspects that would make me better.

With that level of diligence plus the sophisticated training methods employed by Dave Lease, and training with some of the fastest starters in the world (Colin Jackson was widely acknowledged as being the best 60m runner in the world), combined with a sophisticated approach towards power and force-to-weight ratios, led to my becoming, slowly but surely, rejuvenated. With Linford, and Daniel Plummer, I was working on block starts alongside two of the best in the world, and having benefited from the inspirational guidance of Linford Christie over the preceding years I was in a good place mentally and physically.

I never dreamt that these modifications in my regime would have such a powerful effect, and also so quickly. In the summer of 2003, I became British 100m champion, and finished within a whisker of being the 100m World champion at the Stade de France in Paris. Kim Collins (St. Kitts and Nevis), pipped me and Darrel Brown (Trinidad and Tobago), on the line in a blanket photo finish that had to be separated not by hundredths, but by thousandths of seconds. I took bronze but that medal was less than one hundredth of a second from being the gold. Four days later I finished 4th in the 200m and, with the Olympic Games in Athens merely months away, I had cemented myself as one of the top sprinters in the world, in both sprint events.

The tearful Christmas days, the heart-to-hearts on the sand dunes after training, the hours I spent on the sofa feeling depressed and missing my family, felt like an age ago, and to top it all Clair discovered she was pregnant again. Things had gone from being bathed in darkness to being brilliantly bright.

9

Athens

"Darren, you're Olympic champion."
Uchenna Emedolu

Sometimes in life you get what you want, but not the way you want it. I told Mr Law, my teacher at Ashton-on-Mersey School, that I would compete in the Olympic Games. To his credit, he didn't laugh or patronise me. He acknowledged my dream, and supported it. To this extent, he was one of the first people who came to my mind as I was staring at the Olympic gold medal hanging from my neck once the tears had been swept away after the anthem had rung out in Athens. The presence of former training partners, family and friends, served as an emotional reminder of the journey that had taken me from the streets of Manchester to the track in the Greek capital: of the barriers I had to overcome and the help I received to be successful. The cameo role one particular person played during a crucial crossroads in my career came to mind. I just wasn't to know that until years later. It involved my close friend from Sale Racecourse, Lynx.

Early in March 2004, our second son Dillan was born to add greater joy, and responsibility to the Campbell household. Being a father for the first time was a phenomenal experience, but becoming parents for the second time created a deeper sense of family for Clair and me. It also, naturally, brought with it the extra burden for Clair of late nights, feeding, fatigue and the stresses that come with two children under the age of five scampering around the house. Each training session that season was preceded with some extra bottle warming, cooling, feeding, playing, wiping and screaming. At times it felt that single athletes with no kids might as well start three metres ahead of everyone else. I could not be more effusive in my praise towards Clair during this time, as she was utterly fantastic as a mother to Aaryn and Dillan, and highly empathetic as a wife knowing that her husband was a dedicated athlete embarking on an Olympic year.

Prior to the Games a training camp was organised in Cyprus, where Sue Barrett from Nuff Respect management had found a hotel that was clean, serene, and had just opened in a quiet secluded area. Linford, Paul Gray, Daniel Plummer and me all stayed in the same complex, which provided the perfect environment for what we needed, but in the last run of the last training session at the camp I tore my hamstring. Fortunately for me, Bryan English, the UK Athletics doctor, was on hand to treat me two to three times per day, and so was Dr Müller-Wohlfahrt who gave his expertise and time.

The omens, and the general feeling in the build-up to the Olympics, were good, but there were reservations concerning my muscular health. What was meant to be a pre Olympic launch pad achieved little, and only succeeded in creating tension by suggesting things weren't going well. I had learnt the lesson of having trusted individuals around me, and knowing that this would be my final Olympic Games I ensured that plenty of my closest and dearest shared the experience, not only for their benefit but for mine, which is why Lynx and his brother flew out to join me.

During my own sporting journey, coaches, parents and teachers all contributed greatly in cultivating the fertile ground from which grew my success and resulted in my journey to Olympic gold – from my first teacher, David Law, to Linford Christie, my final coach – and I knew it would be crucial to have friends and training partners from my younger days with me at the Olympic Games. I was lucky to have close training partners such as Paul Gray, who had played such a massive part in aiding my training. He enabled me to be judged against the highest standards, day-in day-out, keep me grounded, and give me the confidence that I had done the necessary work. Daniel Plummer was also essential to my development. Without having the good fortune of meeting and training with him – he would demolish me over the first few strides – I would not have acknowledged, so early in my career, that I was a poor starter and needed to improve. I quickly realised that if I could reproduce Paul's technical ability and replicate Daniel's start, powered by the weightlifting introduced to me by Dave Lease, I was sure I would be able to perform to a higher standard and increase the chances of achieving the Olympic success I craved.

The hamstring injury hampered me in the 100m heats, and even though I had qualified for the semi-final of the 200m, the decision had almost been made to withdraw me from the Games. My doctor, Bryan English, and some of his closest professional companions had enough experience and expertise to acknowledge the chasm that existed between my excellent muscular health and the level of performance required at this level.

The fact that I was in the shape of my life was irrelevant, a factor many sportspeople can relate to. There is often a hair's breadth between being in fantastic physical shape, on the 99.99th percentile of your physical ability, and over-reaching to the extent that your body rebels. My body had rebelled. The training had resulted in a huge improvement, performance-wise, but I'd literally stretched the hamstring too far. I was resigned to the situation that my body needed a reboot before going again but it wouldn't be now, and certainly not in Athens, it appeared.

The doctors, coaches and my family, were of the firm opinion that I should be gently persuaded to take a quiet flight home to recuperate and reassess. The hamstring had played a big part in this but, in athletics, it is always treated with suspicion. I was not above calling out my own performances as being poor, but there was a huge frustration bubbling within me with this specific injury. I knew I had run poorly in the heats, but I was in the shape of my life and in a position to run well. It was difficult knowing what to do.

One person who had been in exactly the same position I'd now found myself was my coach, Linford Christie. He gave me valuable insight concerning the importance of embracing doubt, criticism and disparagement. He was able to appreciate such aspects more clearly now, years after they had come knocking at his door. He said many things which made sense to me, and enabled me to view my difficulties from an alternative angle.

He not only bolstered my own confidence by – cheekily and affably – confirming that he had no doubt that I would be the 'next Linford

Christie', but also reinforcing the notion that with all eyes being on me, others may not have been concentrating on themselves. Linford had the ability to share his wisdom in a way that made sense. He was spot on.

He also contrasted this positive reinforcement with a more tempered approach. He reminded me that if I wasn't focused or resolute enough, I would not be able to fully apply myself. If I was to compete, I needed to compartmentalise the noise and the distractions that surrounded me and focus only on the things that would help me. He made me appreciate that a distraction for me could be shifted to being a distraction for others if I was able to rise above the emotion.

Yet a storm was now brewing off the track. I was called out, as being a 'faker', by Michael Johnson on national television with my mother and family watching back home. In hindsight it was a media distraction that was blown out of all proportion, but it's not something you are able to mentally process in real-time. We have since reconciled and have no issues whatsoever. These days we are both clear-headed individuals, not emotionally involved in our own careers as athletes, but things were so different in the testosterone-fuelled alpha male circus of the Olympic Games between two track athletes from Texas and Manchester.

An argument about me having a hamstring injury – or not, in Johnson's opinion – led to a distracting destructive squabble that need not had been raised. It was so controversial that it led to the BBC's commentators, on their large yellow sofas, broadcasting the arguments and counter-arguments live on TV. It was both bitter and acrimonious.

I was livid that the very notion that something as innocuous as a torn hamstring had exploded into a media story because of Michael Johnson, whom I had the ultimate respect for, had suddenly made my walking away from Athens something that could be misconstrued as me opting for an easy exit. Making up excuses for poor performances was not what I, my family, or my coaches were all about.

This incident with Michael changed the goalposts entirely. This wasn't, and isn't, how people in the Campbell family acted when their integrity and honesty were called into question. This is where my family values ultimately provided a reason to continue even though the injury was severe enough to question the wisdom of staying in Greece. Bryan English, the GB team doctor, even sent ultrasound scans to the media to confirm the tear in order to de-escalate what was rapidly becoming a big story, as exemplified by *The Guardian's* David Plummer who, on 27 August 2004, a day before the Olympic 4 x 100m relay final, wrote:

> *'The rancour between the British sprinter Darren Campbell and the BBC's athletics analyst Michael Johnson spilled into a heated confrontation in an Athens nightclub on Wednesday night. Campbell's manager Sue Barrett yesterday alleged that Johnson accused the sprinter of lying over a hamstring injury that Campbell blamed for his failure to qualify for the finals of either the 100 or 200 metres in Athens. Campbell, angered by comments made by the five-times Olympic gold medallist while summarising on BBC, confronted him at a party hosted by MTV. Barrett said: "Darren Campbell told him [Johnson] 'I'm not happy about what you've been saying about me' and Johnson replied 'That's my opinion.' When Darren Campbell said 'Let's get this straight. Are you saying I've been lying about my injury?' Johnson responded 'Yes'. Then he walked away".'*

I knew there was a party, but the truth was I didn't even want to go out. Lynx convinced me, saying I needed to get fresh air and stretch my legs. He kept coming back at me, rationalising that if my hamstring was going to heal and enable me to run, leaving the room for a few hours would serve me well. Conversely, if my Olympic Games were indeed over due to the injury and I was going home anyway, why not experience a bit of Athens? His persuasive nature met my ambivalence and the end result was that we went to the MTV party.

There were many notable individuals from the world of sport and entertainment at the party, including the world heavyweight boxing champion Evander Holyfield. As fate would have it, one of the first people I saw in this open-air party was none other than Michael Johnson himself. I was furious with Michael's attitude, and unfounded opinions on the television. Respected figures in sport are employed as commentators in order to provide a perspective and an opinion, and making comments to enhance what happens is the currency of a good commentator, but Johnson was such a legend of the sport there was no need to tarnish his own reputation by questioning the integrity of a fellow, and highly successful, athlete. That kind of rationale was a million miles away from an Athens nightclub at a celebrity party, however, and my heightened emotions threatened to make me my own worst enemy.

Almost immediately we engaged in conversation about him using his television platform to accuse me of faking injury to hide a poor performance. "Are you calling me a liar or a faker?" I asked him (or words to that effect). "Yes, I think you are," he replied, before turning his back to me.

There would be, I thought, during the next 30 seconds in that nightclub, no other option for me than to show Michael Johnson, through physical violence, how wrong he was and the depth of pain and anger he'd created. Those 30 seconds – and this is no overblown exaggeration – would ultimately define my career, and my life. The decisions I would make would lead to me either being plastered over the front pages of the world's newspapers, for all the wrong reasons, or being written about on their back pages, for all the right reasons. The issue at hand was that my instincts were honed on the estate where I grew up, where there was no fight-or-flight option. Back in those days, if someone hit you, you hit back harder. In sport, acting tough was easy because it never had to be backed up in the same way.

In this instance I felt that the line had been crossed. I was livid due to his accusing me of being a faker, and now turning his back to me. It wouldn't have been beyond the realms of possibility that what happened next could have led to my waking up the following day in an Athens jail, dismissed in disgrace from the UK Athletics team, and quite possibly paying the greatest price of all: watching my teammates win Olympic Gold without me. Michael Johnson has never known, until now, how close he was to feeling the full force of a man raised on the streets of Manchester.

This is where the effect of the decision I made to involve my close friends from home played in my favour. I had friends at my side that evening who had experienced true loss through violence earlier in their lives. Their own threshold of red mist was set at a much higher level through personal experience. I have no doubt that those same friends viewed my talent as a gift, and they were not going to let me lose my chance at success by indulging in what would, essentially, be an act of primal rage that would serve no other purpose than cause trouble. I have no doubt of the importance of having a friend with me

Hanging out after training with Olympic 110m hurdles champion Mark McCoy and Linford.

With Jamie Baulch on the Hollywood Walk of Fame while on a promotional visit to Los Angeles for Puma.

The sprint start: different styles, one intent. Some friendly competition with a host of world class sprinters during a training camp near Sydney.

Athenian's fast ascent defies Campbell charge

The Sydney Olympics 2000. The headline in The Guardian says it all: 'Astonishing burst from an unknown Greek'.

Campbell sprints to silver

Flying Greek's sensational win leaves Sydney stunned

At 30 metres to go I really thought I'd done it. Initially I was devastated, but I had won the silver medal and was very proud of my achievement.

Darren's story of success is a real weepie

CRYING GAME: Campbell is overcome by emotion after finishing second in the 200 metres but his mood quickly turns to delight (inset)

Silver in Sydney for the guy from Sale Racecourse.

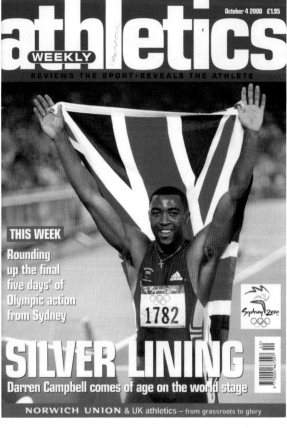

Cover of Athletics Weekly, October 2000.

Mum deserves a medal

THIS is the moment that Marva Campbell finally caught up with her Olympic hero son Darren. And despite their mutual admiration, it WAS just a moment. The Sale Harrier, who won a silver medal in the 200 metres at the Sydney Olympics,

returned to Manchester to film an edition of BBC's A Question of Sport and Marva trapped him at the studios. Darren, 27, who famously declared: 'I always say it is thanks to my mum' within minutes of winning his medal, said yesterday: 'This is

the first time we've been able to see each other since then.' His 17-month-old son Aaryn also joined in the celebrations. Asked if he'd be in Manchester for the Commonwealth Games in 2002 Darren said: 'I might have retired by then.'

Showing the Olympic silver medal to my mum, who had sacrificed so much to support me, and my athletics career, was a very special moment.

The 2002 Commonwealth Games, in Manchester. Leading Team England out for the opening ceremony in my home town was one of my proudest moments. It's a memory I'll treasure forever. (© Phil Cole / Getty Images)

Winning gold in the 4 x 100m. As an Englishman, and a Mancunian, that was a special moment. (© Adrian Dennis / Getty Images)

The 2003 World Championships, in Paris. Winning the bronze in the 100m was one of my finest performances. I surprised everyone, apart from myself. (© Phil Cole / Getty Images)

Team GB also won silver in the 4 x 100m, but the performance was removed from the records and the medals returned after Dwain's drug-taking was discovered. (© Jack Guez / Getty Images)

DREAM OVER

The 2004 Athens Olympics. Myself and Christian were both distraught after failing to reach the 200m final. (© South Wales Argus)

CHARIOTS OF IRE

From JOHN CROSS in Athens

SPRINTER Darren Campbell had a furious eyeball-to-eyeball row with track legend Michael Johnson after his Olympics exit.

Campbell, 30, last in his 200 metres semi-final, was incensed by Johnson's BBC TV criticism, casting doubt on his thigh injury.

Johnson, a Games champion at 200 and 400, had claimed: "I'm confused...no one questions his talent, but this time he wasn't in shape."

Early yesterday Campbell, below left, met Johnson in an Athens nightclub and said: "I'm not happy about what you have been saying."

Johnson, 36, replied: "That is my opinion." The pair had a further bitter exchange and were then dragged apart by security staff.

FULL STORY: PAGES 8&9

Michael Johnson's comments about my performance, and the extent of my injury, infuriated me and hit the headlines (Daily Mirror above left and right), but I managed to keep my composure and focus on the relay.

After some poor technical performances from Team GB at previous finals, everything clicked that day in Athens. We ran the perfect race, which is what we needed to beat the impressive Americans. Our team spirit was immense - we ran for each other, not as individuals. (© Bob Thomas / Getty Images)

Hero is thrilled to be home

ATHENS 2004

NEWPORT'S golden champion, Darren Campbell, is happy to be back at home with his young family after his stunning Olympic victory.

He was reunited with partner Clair Jacobs and their children, five-year-old Aaryn, and Dillon, aged five months.

Darren was parted from his family for pre-Olympic training in Cyprus and then during the Athens games, but returned in triumph yesterday.

"I am glad to be back home and back in Wales," said the 31-year-old hero, who has lived in Rogerstone for a number of years.

He won his gold medal as part of Great Britain's amazing relay team who snatched the coveted top spot from under the noses of the favourites, the USA foursome.

The victory was especially sweet for Darren, who had failed to make the 100m or 200m final after being hindered by injury.

He was able to prove to those who had criticised his earlier performances that he is one of the country's greatest sprinters.

GOLDEN DAYS: Olympic champion Darren Campbell, happy to be home with partner Clair Jacobs and children Aaryn, five, and Dillon, five months

Picture: MIKE LEWIS

Taking an Olympic gold medal back to Clair, Dillon and Aaryn in Newport meant the world to me. (© Mike Lewis / South Wales Argus)

Darren Campbell, the boy from Moss Side, became Darren Campbell MBE, the gold medal-winning Olympian at Buckingham Palace. It was a day the two of us will never forget.

The 2006 European Championships, in Gothenburg. Receiving the baton from Dwain Chambers on way to gold in the 4 x 100m, but this victory generated no elation within me: in fact, the very opposite emotion. Every member of the team did their job brilliantly, but I felt empty inside. (© Julian Finney / Getty Images)

I've taken a strong line against drugs in sport (and society) throughout my life, and I simply couldn't reconcile those principles with the reality of winning the gold medal. I opted out of the post-race lap of honour and felt even more uncomfortable during the medal ceremony: sadly, the last one I'd ever experience. (© Michael Steele / Getty Images)

After retirement I used my knowledge of sprint training to good use in football and rugby, including with Sale Sharks (L-R) James Gaskell, Will Addison and Neil Briggs. I was to coach James again during my time at Wasps. (© Getty Images)

With my old friend, Linford, I got involved with, and really enjoyed, the Street Athletics project. If memory serves me right, she beat me in a photo finish! (© Getty Images)

With Katherine Merry, a dear friend and long-time training partner, in China supporting a Team GB Youth Championships. (© Getty Images)

Fronting a charity event with Jason Gardener, John Regis, Iwan Thomas and Roger Black. (© Getty Images)

Involvement with the Street Athletics project and helping people to discover the joys of athletics was hugely enriching and very satisfying. (© Getty Images)

Having fun with Linford at a media event. (© Getty Images)

A wonderful actor and a lovely person. With Don Cheadle at a party in Los Angeles.

With Martin Offiah – a true rugby legend – while filming Superstars.

With Audley Harrison and Lennox Lewis at Audley's wedding in Jamaica. I'm over 6ft but these guys are big!

It was a real pleasure to appear on Soccer AM with Helen Chamberlain.

Fellow Mancunian, Ricky Hatton – a brilliant boxer and a great friend.

Darren Campbell examines what inspires, motivates and encourages people in sport, and what you can do to follow them

I was very nervous at first, but I really enjoy broadcasting with BBC 5Live. (© BBC)

Pro-Athlete-Supplementation; my business and passion. I'm so lucky to have such a great team working with me. They are an essential part of our success. (© PAS)

Clair and me celebrating our wedding: with (L-R) Dillon and Aaryn.

Happy times with Clair, to whom I owe so much.

Dillon, Leoni and Aaryn – at school and on holiday – I could not be prouder of my children

All the family (including Marva, Linwal and Jessica) celebrating my sister Sophia's graduation, as a teacher, from Manchester Metropolitan University. We are all incredibly proud of her academic success.

I love my family so much, and feel blessed to have recovered from such a serious illness. It has taught me to cherish every single day I spend with them.

that night who had the experience of seeing the dangers and pitfalls of emotional violence, and who was immediately aware of the warning signs, and decided to act on my behalf.

"Are you really going to let Michael Johnson destroy everything that you have built up until this point?" asked Lynx. "If it's that serious I'll do it for you."

If seeing a champagne bottle clatter Michael Johnson would make me feel better, a close friend was willing to do it, and also take the punishment for it. At that point, I realised the seriousness of the situation and snapped out of it. I suddenly needed to protect Lynx, from his wish to protect me. He had processed the threat and dismantled the situation in seconds. His appreciation of the situation and his ability to deal with it in that way would not, in reality, have happened if I'd been with a staff member of UK Athletics, or a security attaché from the Olympics.

I left the nightclub emotionally charged, but with a renewed determination. I decided there and then that I would call representatives from UK Athletics and ask them for a meeting. Having people with me who I knew and trusted was so emotionally comforting in what I knew would be my last Olympic Games. It could have been so very different for me were it not for the intervention, not of a coach or an official, but of someone on my wavelength. Someone who knew me as a friend, not as an athlete.

I loved how emotionally involved the people around me were in my journey, and I embraced it. I discovered that the people around you celebrated your successes more joyously than you did. They lived your failures and successes with you. Sport is far more than the individual athlete and the decisions they make. If you don't care deeply and passionately about how your performances affect those around you, you won't be as emotionally invested in your own success either. Respect for others, mutual love, and a great desire to see smiles on the faces of your support team, friends and family can lead to an over-reach beyond your wildest dreams. It certainly did for me.

Over many years I'd kept the same team of masseurs, coaches and doctors who had laid the solid foundations of my success. These were people I trusted, and who, in turn, trusted me. They also felt the sting and the anger of the hamstring 'alibi' being touted as a credible story as much as I did, maybe more so.

People such as my masseur 'Longy' (Duy Long Nguyen) – although given the fact that he had worked with such luminaries as Keanu Reeves and Elle MacPherson among many others, I cannot claim him as solely mine – who had gone over and above the call of duty in helping me out. During the Sydney Olympics, and despite being incredibly busy, he fitted me into his schedule to receive vital treatment and obtained a pass to get into the warm-up area where I was. It was no ordinary pass. He had persuaded Rupert Murdoch to lend it to him.

Longy also helped me in Athens. The fact that this was to be done on Frank Lowy's $110m luxury yacht which was moored in the glorious waters around Athens made the gesture even more special. While lying on this boat and gazing at the stars, I remember thinking, 'If I do win Olympic gold what a crazy story it would be.' Frank Lowy, businessman and shopping centre magnate, has to be one of the most fascinating people I have ever met. Born in Czechoslovakia to Jewish parents, his family fled to Hungary during the Second World War. While living in hiding in the ghetto – at a time when other families in hiding were being discovered and shot – his father caught a train one day, never to return. Frank later learnt that he had been murdered at the Auschwitz concentration camp. Upon emigrating to Australia after the war, he set up the shopping centres business, the Westfield Corporation, and became one of the richest men in the world. It was through Duy Long Nguyen that our respective paths crossed and while I was by no stretch of the imagination one of Longy's most high-end clients, he treated me as one. This kind of benevolence made me humble and gracious that others did things for me that I didn't believe I had earned. I wanted to repay them by sharing these special occasions with them. I believed they had earned it.

The dynamic of this support network that I adored, trusted and believed in, played its part. Had just one of them taken a different view on the narrative and not felt as involved or attached to the situation, this could easily have led to doubt creeping in to the decision-making process. As it happened, the professionalism, hard work, sheer dedication and integrity of the people surrounding me led to one small win following another.

Hours on the physio bed with Longy led to an improved range of motion. This led to the ability to train a little and suddenly the dynamic of this Olympic Games started changing. A little gleam of light appeared each day thereafter, and was a catalyst for even more determination, positivity and a can-do mentality from everyone in the support network. The *modus operandi* became 'we might not succeed in this but if we fail, we'll fail trying our hardest'.

The amount of focus and drive that attitude generated became infectious. Having the calibre of professionals such as doctors Hans Müller-Wolfahrt and Bryan English on my side, fuelling my confidence and providing support meant that their words carried weight. I trusted their opinions not only because of the fact they were – and are – respected as the finest in the world but also because they had invested their time and energy in me. It is hard to convey what this means to an athlete surrounded by deep inner doubt and anxiety. When people believe in you, you tend to believe in yourself. It was almost like a distress call was given out, and all these people came to help me.

The relay quartet decided to hold a meeting, at which we were all open and candid with one another. I explained that the previous few days had been the most emotionally painful days of my professional career, and that despite my problems and injury I was ready to run, or ready to go home, depending on the team's opinion. I did state, however, to everyone's agreement, that I felt confident we could beat the Americans. I felt that we could pressure them into a mistake and then pounce to take gold. I held the opinion that we would either go home medal-less – by over-exerting, making an error, or simply by injury – or we could win gold and shock the world.

I told them that I wanted to run and give it everything, even if it meant damaging my hamstring, but I was also ready to go home for the team if that was the collective decision. I also said that if they decided to back me, and my hamstring went again during the race, it would be totally wrong for them to say to the press that I shouldn't have run. If we won, we'd win as a team, but if we came last, we'd come last as a team. One decision, as one group, for one race, for one purpose.

The decision was unanimous. I was in. Following that meeting, I knew that we were going to win Olympic gold. We had created an unbreakable emotional bond and we were willing to risk everything for one another. Jason was going to hunt down the Americans on the first bend, I was going to put pressure on their second changeover by breathing down their necks, Marlon was going to give Mark a lead with a scintillating last bend, and Mark was going to roar to gold tearing down the home straight knowing the Americans would be inches behind him. We had it all mapped out.

It was now 6pm, and as we approached the warm-up track by the Olympic Stadium the words of American sprinter Maurice Greene buzzed around my head: "It takes four to win, and if something goes wrong for one, it goes wrong for all of us." How right he was.

Three members of the British team had learned vital lessons at the Olympics four years previously. Marlon, Jason and me had all been mentally scarred by the mistakes made at the highest level, and lost everything. Having been a part of a so-called podium-certain team, we were now three-quarters of an underdog team. In contrast, the statement from Maurice, one of the world's greatest ever sprinters and one of the quartet who were overwhelming favourites for the gold, suggested an all-for-one musketeer mindset, where success or failure would be shared by a band of inseparable brothers.

The reality, as we stepped on to the warm-up track in Athens on that hot sticky evening was that the American team, this supposed band of brothers, weren't even warming up together. In an event that required the synchronicity of an orchestra without a conductor, it didn't escape our notice that the string section of America were tuning up separately to the woodwind section, so to speak.

Having experienced failure twice previously, we Brits were paranoid that the slightest, most miniscule element of disharmony might affect our chances. The USA team on the other hand were now fragmented into what were essentially separate, rival sprint camps, reflecting the culture in the USA of coach/athlete camps. The individual parts were so strong, the collective whole was overlooked because everyone knew that they were going to win. Including, it seemed, the American quartet.

I was privileged to be the men's team captain for these Games but, while stretching and doing my own preparatory drills alongside my teammates, I was conscious that I was potentially about to head home from an Olympic Games as captain of the first ever British men's team not to have won a single medal, of any colour.

This kind of thing didn't usually weigh heavily on my mind, but I was aware that after the previous two Games – particularly the outcomes of the respective relays – it would add more fuel to the firestorm of criticism that was awaiting the British team back home following such an underwhelming performance. This, for me, would be the final event of the final day of my own final Olympic Games.

Seeing the US team alongside us on the warm-up track, oozing a cool, effortless confidence, revealed the contrasting approaches of the two teams. While the Americans came across as nonchalant we were totally focussed, having prepared with painstaking precision and an obsessive attention to detail. We were, in this respect, the beneficiaries of previous failures. With Dwain Chambers' results being annulled, the GB men's sprint relay squad was instantly relegated to being ranked 15th in the world. This was significant because only 16 teams would qualify for the Olympic Games, so the team literally was teetering on the brink of complete exclusion. This low ranking was artificial and unrepresentative of the reality of how good we were, but it was the situation in which we found ourselves. Because of this, we had to obtain qualifying times in events prior to the Games.

This was a scenario born from anguish. I had lost a medal because of the annulment of performances, and many of us were extremely bitter at the ignominy of having to enter qualification races, where I'm sure many others were laughing behind our backs at how far British relay sprinting had fallen. What was increasingly evident, though, was that in this quest to qualify we had been practising, improving, refining and smoothing the edges. Through this process which had been forced upon us, we were moulding a team bred through loss, frustration, determination and with absolutely nothing to lose.

At the Atlanta Games eight years previously, the occasion, the excitement, and the distractions blurred the senses. The sensations I experienced while walking over to the relay box meant I was outside 'the moment' due to the nervous energy surrounding me. These things had been key to my downfall so I knew they could also affect others in the same way, and I was convinced that I could illicit mistakes in others. I would make it my mission to ensure that Justin Gatlin, my American rival on the back straight – knowing the gaze of millions of expectant American eyes would be focused on him – would be overcome by the nerves he had been trying to suppress.

It didn't involve any words, just body language. A look of desolation on my part, a hard blowing of the cheeks, and a 1,000-yard stare directly towards him. These would all act as cues to create a 'rope-a-dope' act based on getting him to think just a little bit harder about the scenes all around him instead of the task at hand. A shake of the head and a suggestion of a smile would also let him know that we all knew the effusion of confidence that he displayed betrayed the nervous anxiety he would most certainly be feeling.

The GB team needed to crank up the tension, in the knowledge that tension can make things unravel very quickly. Being trained, and being experienced, was on our side due to the number of times we had performed as a quartet. We weren't as quick as the Americans so we needed to use everything else at our disposal. We weren't perfect. In fact we had already made mistakes in the semi-final when Mark Lewis-Francis and I had exchanged our baton in the nick of time, but this, if anything, emphasised the strategy of being able to steal crucial milliseconds away from the other teams by forcing mistakes on them.

It was 7.04pm and the British quartet was now trackside. Seeing Dame Kelly Holmes win gold, and the exhilaration she radiated in the immediate aftermath was special. She embraced us trackside prior to our own Olympic final race and filled us with the belief that we, too, could strive for that moment in our lives. I genuinely feel that the timing of Kelly's win added an extra impetus to us at a crucial time. It was when we were mentally preparing to enter the arena, and seeing a good friend and colleague achieve her life's goal right in front of us instilled a desire deep in our stomachs that this could also be our time.

Kelly was a calculated, earnest competitor with controlled aggression flowing through her performances, but to see her body language and her facial expressions seconds after winning Olympic gold was phenomenal. I may be completely wrong in this assessment, as those moments – as I was to find out minutes later – evaporate into the cosmos in a cloud of emotions while you are experiencing them, but Dame Kelly's visceral support so soon after her triumph really resonated with us. She was desperate for us to experience the same sheer exhilaration she had just enjoyed. Her instinctive, aggressive, yet totally appropriate encouragement was so emotional and absolutely sincere. She had just savoured her life-changing moment and was now imploring us to achieve the same for ourselves.

It was during these moments when I realised that even track and field can be a team sport. In her moment of ecstasy she was thinking of the next race and her Team GB teammates, and channelling her support through tearful happiness. This form of encouragement instilled belief, and because of the circumstances – and the source of the encouragement – it truly meant something. Had Kelly not won gold, or even a medal, and given us the same form of encouragement, it might not have meant as much.

It was now 7.32pm and we were making our final preparations at our individual start positions. Many describe the night they win Olympic gold as a special particularly as the start of the event approaches. They recall a buzz, a crackling of energy in the stadium like an intangible electricity. Perhaps special nights elicit special, indefinable feelings and it certainly felt special for the four of us as we walked out on to the track in Athens. Even though the stands weren't that full because local interest had waned after the Greek athletes Kenteris and Thanou had withdrawn, the British quartet were determined to put on a show the crowds would never forget.

Getting a good start would be crucial, and the body language of most of the lead runners was tense as the starter called the teams to the blocks. The nerves were heightened when there was a false start. There was the possibility, from my vantage point behind the hammer cage on the first bend, that it was Jason. More delays. More distraction. More time for minds to wander and lose concentration. It indeed was Jason, and he was on a warning, so even more pressure. Thanks to Jason's false start, the tension increased exponentially.

As I paced up and down the back straight, I was conscious that I would know what Justin Gatlin and Maurice Greene would be thinking as they lined up for the restart a minute or so later. They would be edgy and frustrated – thinking they should already be celebrating their win, not setting up again to start the race – which creates a heightened anxiety to get it over and done with. We, on the other hand, had all the time in the world. Our goal was to simply to stay in the race, and to give Mark Lewis-Francis on the last leg some semblance of a chance to win.

A long line of mistakes, failures, and frustrations had been slowly simmering on our collective back burner, conspiring to give us the greatest day of our lives. Thanks to Dwain and his performances being scratched, we were through the qualifying process, highly tuned and highly practised. Thanks to Michael Johnson and his negative comments on my 'faking', I was furious and focused. Thanks to two previous failures in two consecutive Games, the team had experienced how the distractions of the occasion could affect anyone. Thanks to the possibility of having to leave the Games without a single men's medal – especially having seen Dame Kelly Holmes' gold half an hour previously – we were very motivated; and now, finally, thanks to Jason's false start ramping up the tension to boiling point, the other teams were primed for a mistake. None of these things involved us running faster but they all contributed in their own individual ways to our team gold. All these failures, mistakes and negative experiences had surrounded us, so there was no reason why a few wouldn't creep into the Americans' sphere. That, at least, was the hope.

This was it. The Olympic men's 4 x 100m final. Bang! The Bath Bullet exploded as soon as the crack of the starting gun reverberated through the stadium. Despite his false start, Jason's initial few strides were exceptionally quick and powerful. I started my initial preparation as soon as I saw Jason closing in around the bend, rubbing my hands to ensure the dryness and stickiness was there ready to receive the baton. This was my time to shine. At this moment, I could sense tension in the American ranks when it was apparent that the recently crowned Olympic 200m champion Shawn Crawford was not out-running the stagger and pulling away from his competitors, which would have been expected from the bend specialist. This would not have been on the Americans' script.

The changeover between Jason and me was smooth. Even though Shawn Crawford had caught up with the lane outside, Justin Gatlin was by no means in full stride when taking the baton. My thoughts were completely clear at this point, with no hesitation or complexity, just a total focus on executing my role. The back straight instantly became a haven of tranquillity, with the crowd noise evaporating into the night sky and just the footsteps of my fellow athletes and their panting breaths as company.

My eyes were completely transfixed on my teammate Marlon, a full 100 metres away. The back straight was like a long highway stretching out far into the distance, with the figure of Marlon breaking through the haze on the horizon. I ran those ten seconds in total calmness and composure, the polar opposite to the previous two Olympics where I was full of tension and anxiety having put myself under huge, unrelenting pressure to perform.

ATHENS

The experience of those ten seconds still stays with me to this day as a feeling, not a memory. I can still relate to the hardness of my ankles punching the floor, the taste of my saliva, the weight of my spinal muscles tensing hard and absorbing every step as my legs propelled me forward on a track that suddenly felt so sympathetic and inviting to run on.

With about 30 metres to go, and with all the athletes now in full view, I became very calm indeed for I could see and sense the anxiety in the lane outside me. Justin Gatlin was cruising, setting himself for the change of baton, and Coby Miller, his American teammate, had set off well, probably too well. He was away like a gazelle, but didn't synchronise with Gatlin's approach which created the doubt, the mis-timing, the stutter that we all knew was possible.

I handed the baton to Marlon as smoothly as it had been passed to me by Jason. Our baton probably didn't change speed in the slightest, going from my hand to his, whereas Coby Miller now had to apply the brakes and re-start his engine to avoid running out of the exchange zone, baton-less. That sequence of events: Jason's brilliant start, the smooth changeovers, my decent back straight, and the American team's mistake saw the pressure transfer from us to them. That final should have been the occasion for the American quartet to shine, but the errors that had plagued the British team for the previous 12 years now jumped two lanes. Coby Miller had a poor exchange, and the last thing I saw before watching Marlon's heels flutter away into the distance was the American trying to make up for his error by pushing too hard and losing the fluidity which is essential for speed. Gatlin and Miller had still run phenomenal times for their relay legs, but their baton had experienced an altogether bumpy stop-start ride and Marlon was gone. This was PERFECT.

Marlon ran the bend of his life. Whether he was aware of it or not, he was closing in on the Nigerians and leaving the Americans in his wake. The balance, grace and raw speed that he demonstrated while keeping his perfect running form was in contrast to the aggression, bouncing shoulders, and tension in the lanes all around him. He was running like a man determined to make his rivals pay for their mistakes. He maintained his posture perfectly, with Nureyev-like elegance, in the middle of his lane and leaning into the home straight ready to put his British quartet in the lead on the last leg of an Olympic final.

At this point the emotion and the tension of the occasion returned to me. I could now hear the noise and sensed the anticipation. As soon as Marlon sped away I slowed to a walk, then fell to my knees and prayed, trying to stay calm as the nerves, tension and anxiety threatened to overwhelm me. The calmness that I had enjoyed during my leg, the focus and the decreased sensory awareness, was replaced by a deafening roar and it was as if every muscle in my body was now granite hard. Since I was no longer in control of the outcome, my brain started sending the same messages that had registered in previous – failed – Olympic relays, and the doubts and fears flooded back as I watched the final stage of the race.

As we had imagined it, Mark Lewis-Francis was now chasing his dreams down the home straight, with Maurice Greene breathing down his neck. Maurice, when in full flight, would have normally eased past the majority of the world's sprinters, but he was now desperately chasing, and chasing is different to sprinting. Mark's determination to hold him off was monumental. His eyes were bulging with desire and his legs pumping piston-like with effort. With both athletes dipping, it was the thickness of Mark's vest that gave us gold.

On the sum of such immeasurables are titles sometimes decided: the hesitation from the false start, the approach of Gatlin to the exchange zone, the stutter between Miller and Gatlin, and the pressure applied by Mark being inside the stagger and ahead of Maurice. Taken individually, these errors would, quite probably, still have resulted in an American gold medal, but when combined as a series of sprint relay imperfections, they resulted in a gold for Team GB.

It was just at this point that Nigerian sprinter Uchenna Emedolu tapped me on the shoulder and said to me with love and respect: "Darren, you're Olympic champion." I was nervously jog-dancing somewhere between the back straight and the water jump as confusion reigned. I could see Mark fist pumping and celebrating, yet there was a period of a few seconds before the stadium screen proclaimed us the men's 4 x 100m relay Olympic Champions. Not the USA. Us. The British quartet.

The other athletes in the relay knew what we, as a team, had been through at previous major finals, and there was a recognition that if we perfected everything on the day we could create a tremor large enough to shake the Parthenon.

ATHENS

Marlon, Jason and Mark were aware of their own talents and the four of us had grown and developed as a team together. We were united in our belief in the others' talents, as well as our team's character and mental fortitude. We were also united in the view that none of the other teams had the unity, drive and togetherness that we had – borne through failing and learning about ourselves in the process.

In those circumstances anything was possible, and in the words of the BBC commentator Steve Cram merely five seconds after the race: "I said anything could happen, but you know what? .... I didn't think it would be ... a gold medal .... for Britain."

In Athens, I had torn my hamstring, taken a beating in the media, been accused of being a faker, fallen out with Michael Johnson, and then won an Olympic gold medal. Sometimes in life you get what you want, just not the way you want it.

10

Retirement

"Mum – I want to change my name. I don't want to be Darren Grant any more. I want to be Darren Campbell."

Darren Andrew Campbell was an Olympic Gold medallist. The realisation of what I'd achieved vindicated the decision I had made when I was nearly 13 years old. A decision that had nothing to do with sport.

I had been nominated for an award at a young sports person of the year ceremony in Manchester, and there was an uncomfortable silence in the car as we were driving home – I'm sure Mum's intuition alerted her to the fact that I had something on my mind. It was at this point that I dropped the bombshell. I wanted to change my name. Mum, far from being surprised or shocked, was more bemused. My personal rationale for such a drastic action revolved around the fact that one day, I was going to go to the Olympics and be famous. Darren Grant – as I was then – had by that time become good friends with the British high-jumper Dalton Grant, who became a big brother figure to me during my early athletics years. He was no relation, but Dalton had surely become rather inquisitive of this 'other' D Grant creating waves on the British athletics scene. Dalton took me under his wing and looked after me, for which I have always been grateful.

In changing my last name to Campbell, I wanted Mum's side of the family to bask in the glory that came with the name. I wanted Mum to have ownership of my successes. Little did either of us know, of course, that such a lofty and unlikely eventuality would come to pass, but I was a determined child with huge ambition. Changing my name – and practising the autograph, of course – was the first step to creating a self-fulfilling prophecy.

Back then, I was spending a lot of time with my granddad over at my grandparents' home. A wise man and a very hard worker, he had reached a point in his life where he was now the proud owner of a house with both a garden and a driveway. This, to me, was as much of a life achievement as winning the Olympics. My uncle – another Campbell – was also becoming successful in his career, in the world of finance, and I simply wanted to confirm my identity as a Campbell and be a part of the family lineage. I told my mum that I wanted all my achievements in the future to honour her and my grandparents. To her credit, my mother agreed and just over a decade and a half later the Campbells could include sporting success on their family roll of honour.

Before I retired I was looking to apply the lessons I had learnt in my career further afield, with the added bonus of having the huge burden of achieving my life's dreams lifted from my shoulders. I had failed to capitalise on my success at the 2000 Sydney Olympic Games, and I had watched the 2001 World Athletics Championships – held in Edmonton, Canada – as an injured couch potato feeling sorry for myself. I was determined that the same wouldn't happen this time. 2004 was a golden year, but my attitude now was 'look out 2005'.

Well, that was the attitude in public. The truth was, I had reached the pinnacle of my career. Having been deprived of a gold medal by a Greek athlete at the Sydney Games, there was a certain irony in my leaving Greece with a sprint gold. Walking through the security gate at Eleftherios Venizelos International Airport in Athens, I placed, along with my passport, phone and wallet, an Olympic gold medal in one of those horizontal grey plastic boxes to be scanned as carry-on luggage for the plane journey home. It was surreal enough to be presented one on the Olympic podium, but a different kind of reality hit me when I presented it, as my own property, to an airport security guard. My recollection was that he was so 'in the zone' looking for dubious materials that he didn't even notice it.

As a 32-year-old, there was now contentment where there used to be impatience. This change of attitude might have yielded better results for some but, for me, I always needed the competitive drive to propel me forward. I had shown that a boy from Sale Racecourse could realise his wildest dreams. The fact that I also had a wonderful wife and two lovely children at home meant there was a permanent smile on my face.

Proving that a middle-aged man from Newport could maintain that same dream didn't quite have the same ring to it somehow. Nevertheless, I was still an athlete, and each training session was still approached with diligence and application. The primal drive and ambition, however, had been tempered. The 2005 season ended up being a hangover of sorts. Not in a post-party sense, but in respect of acknowledging that I had now achieved what I had long desired. Maybe this was the time to start planning my route to retirement. I had spent my entire life with a single-minded purpose, to achieve, and once those achievements had been delivered, and the sacrifices I'd made were now justified, it was time to exhale.

Yet, even in this time of reflection and rest, one of the most phenomenally surreal experiences of my life occurred the morning when I received the news that I was to be awarded an MBE in the 2005 New Year's Honours list. The pride that swept through the Campbell household was enormous. We weren't the type of people who were meant to go to Buckingham Palace: maybe to the Tower of London, but not the Palace. The son of a Jamaican immigrant, born and raised in a crime-infested area of deprivation, didn't expect to be honoured by the Queen. I owed a huge debt of gratitude to a lot of people who'd supported by athletics career, but the MBE felt like the final seal of approval of the way that I, supported by my mum, my grandparents, my friends and my family, had achieved my success. It felt like a vindication of our decision to refuse the opportunities to cheat our way through life. The sacrifices we'd made to keep to the straight and narrow were now all worthwhile.

Back on the track, Helsinki was hosting the big track and field event of 2005, the World Championships, and there was no need for me to work on my finish, or indeed my Finnish: I hadn't qualified. As it transpired, the British team only managed to make a minimal impression on proceedings. Marlon Devonish and Jason Gardener, my fellow relay gold-medallists, were edged out of qualifying for the final of the 100m, and both Marlon and Christian Malcolm missed out on the 200m final. Paula Radcliffe won a fine gold in the marathon, but despite the men's and women's relay teams picking up bronzes it seemed the post-Olympic hangover wasn't just confined to the Campbell household. Sports people often have the indescribable notion of having 'their year' when things go well, and the opposite is also true, when you are just not performing. 2005 wasn't my year.

2006 saw my mojo return, and its return was most welcome. It was almost certainly linked to two events: I was sure I was going to retire that year, and our wonderful daughter Leoni was born. It felt, simultaneously, like the start of something and the end of something. I qualified for the Commonwealth Games in Melbourne but was disqualified in the 200m heats for running out of my lane. In retrospect I wasn't firing on all cylinders. The Games were held so early in the year (March) it was essentially still cross country and winter preparation season. My engine often took a long time to warm up.

A few months after the Commonwealth Games, the 2006 European Championships – which as a competition had been a great source of joy for me over the years – were held in the wonderful and scenic Swedish city of Gothenburg. Despite my rapidly advancing years, and even accounting for the fact that I had already started to entertain many post-career activities from coaching to business-building, I had managed to qualify for the 4 x 100m relay team. I had started the sports supplements company and made inroads into coaching, but I was still, first and foremost, an athlete. In life, and in athletics, I always liked to be prepared in order to finish strongly, and this was no different. A gold medal in a 4 x 100m would serve as the perfect swansong to my career.

The team consisted of Dwain, Marlon, Mark and me. Dwain was on the road back to athletics success and regaining credibility as a major force in the sport. Marlon, always the quiet unassuming gentleman, had won bronze in the individual 200m a few days earlier and was running as well as he'd ever done during his career. His technical ability as an athlete – he was such an elegant runner to watch – and his calmness in all circumstances ensured that he would retire as a highly decorated sportsman. Mark Lewis-Francis had been targeted and unfairly maligned by some media commentators as an unfulfilled talent, yet, as a Commonwealth, European and Olympic gold medallist as well as a double bronze medallist at World Championships, his achievements spoke for themselves. Was he laid back? Of course.

Could he have achieved more? Maybe, but he had developed the knack of anchoring relay teams to gold – a priceless asset for any quartet.

The four of us proved our worth in Gothenburg. We performed well and took the gold medal – seeing off the challenge from the strong French team and the ever-consistent Polish quartet – albeit in a relatively modest time. As soon as Mark crossed the line, finger aloft, Dwain and Marlon were already grabbing flags from the crowd, intent on making their way round to start a lap of honour. As this was happening I tried to read the body language of my teammates to see if this was something that we were indeed going to do, but as I jogged gingerly over towards the finish line – having run the back straight on the second leg of the relay – I was overwhelmed with an intense feeling that this wasn't right, I simply felt incredibly uncomfortable with what this victory meant. I was, of course, overjoyed with us winning the gold medal, but I felt huge reservations about joining the others in a lap of honour. Three of us – Mark, Marlon and me – had already won Olympic gold two years previously in Athens, which didn't diminish the feat of being European champions, but I wasn't as carried away with the elation as I would have been previously. I was content but didn't feel the urge to celebrate.

I had already forfeited a European Championship gold medal as well as a World Championship silver medal because of Dwain's previous transgressions. So, in the circumstances, celebrating with a lap of honour felt inappropriate. I instinctively felt that I was going to regret taking part in the lap of honour more than I was going to regret not doing so. It wasn't about a protest against Dwain's return to athletics. I felt he deserved a second chance after showing contrition for what he'd done. I was simply protesting against a system that allowed those who had corrupted Dwain to get away scot-free. Whitewashing anyone's reputation or pretending that everything was fine wasn't my style. I was frustrated because I knew I was signing off on my own career with a gold medal, but that it was going to end like this. We had won another gold but, since I was relatively sure that it would be my last, I wanted to blend into the background and enjoy it and avoid any conflict with my conscience, which regarded it as a victory for those who should have been exposed and punished.

Several comments from fellow athletes and commentators came my way regarding my actions, none of which addressed the issue at hand. These comments and judgements were themselves wrapped in a myriad of contexts and agendas; none particularly sinister, but all easily rationalised. Michael Johnson expressed surprise at my reaction. Michael and I obviously had a delicate history culminating in the Athens 'faking' comments, so I believe when it came to me, his vision was always going to be clouded. Michael insinuated that if I knew of people who needed to be exposed as facilitators of cheats, I shouldn't have hidden behind track-tantrums or innuendos. I should have named names, he said, so that everyone knew what and whom I was protesting about. That, of course, was impossible because naming someone, even as a suspected cheat, without indisputable evidence is slander, and defamation of character.

John Regis, the 1990 European 200m champion, drew a parallel with Linford and essentially called me a hypocrite: "You can't say no to Dwain when your own coach has failed a drugs test." Perhaps John was merely protecting his athlete, since Dwain had previously been represented by John Regis' management company. To add a little more flavour to the feud, Chambers had previously been managed by - Linford Christie's management company. Let's say there wasn't much straight shooting going on.

My decision not to run a lap of honour and show my discontentment, despite having my own motivations for doing so, ended up being exploited as a vehicle for multiple personal agendas and behind-the-scenes point-scoring. It was exhausting. The following day I was flown to Beijing as a guest of Aviva for a series of media events but found myself having to give over 100 press interviews, with only one subject being raised. I spent most of the time clarifying and justifying my position which was a distraction from the real reason of me being there.

This was when I knew my career was over. I just got tired. My mind and body were already telling me that they were ready for the next thing in life, and it wasn't going to be using all my emotional and physical energy to focus on competitive running. What happened next was a surprise. I started to become nostalgic about my experiences as an athlete before I had even finished. I found myself becoming more appreciative of how lucky I had been in rubbing shoulders with masters of the sport, and having had the opportunity to immerse myself in a *Boy's Own* existence over the previous two decades. My athletics career had taken me on many divergent paths, but each one had taught me so much and I learnt which of them I could apply to benefit my future.

While living in Wales during the early part of my career I had learnt, from the likes of Nigel Walker and Colin Jackson, the importance of planning and attention to detail. Colin had always been a source of inspiration, and witnessing his forensic attitude to self-improvement at such an embryonic stage in my career was fortuitous. I respected Colin so much as an athlete and was so in awe of him that there was an element of distance in our relationship to begin with, as I saw him as occupying a tall, unreachable pedestal. As soon as we matured as individuals, though, I would like to think that we became friends rather than training partners and he held me in as high a regard as I held him. Coming from the land of Dylan Thomas and a nation whose highest honours are awarded to its bards for creating magic with words, it was fitting that Colin's hurdling technique was poetic in its perfection. I had been so lucky and privileged to witness the hours he spent behind the scenes honing his athletic artistry. Colin's career coincided with hurdling super-heavyweights such as Greg Foster, Roger Kingdom and Allen Johnson – yet he beat them all, consistently.

I also became thankful that I had enjoyed the tutelage of a great mentor in Linford Christie. He had been able to relay to me, first-hand, the realities of being the best in the world, and of dominating a sport. I secretly revelled in the fact that Linford had a love-hate relationship with the media, to the extent that these relationships alone generated column inches. I had been born on the streets where strength and posturing solved conflicts, and Linford oozed strength, posture and conflict. When Linford prowled around the starting line you knew he could both beat the other athletes in the sprint to the tape, and beat them in a fight if he had to. I loved that. I respected the fact that he pushed me to my limits, and know, and hope deep down that he knows, I still love him for it. Linford will go down in history as one of the greatest names ever in British sport but, more importantly for me and my family, he will go down as one of the key reasons that I was able to fulfil my life's dream. That, to me, means more than being able to simply recite his first name alongside Daley or Mo as British sporting superstars who will forever be recognised by just their first names.

The same applies to Denise Lewis. During the Atlanta Olympics in 1996, when her honesty crushed my arrogance, Denise was already a British sporting icon who had achieved so much with such great dignity and humility. I, however, was a medal-less Mancunian with an overconfident, and as yet unearned, swagger. She was a presence in British athletics whose gravitas sent a message to all other ambitious athletes that there was someone amongst them who upheld the highest standards. In any team sport she would have been the captain, the figurehead that all others looked to for guidance and direction. I was forever grateful that she gave me both. I think I truly knew I had earned the credibility I desired as an athlete when I knew Denise Lewis respected me.

My training teammates over the years – Daniel Plummer, Paul Gray, Jamie Baulch, Katharine Merry, Emily Maher, Matt Shirvington and Matt Elias – were not only outstanding athletes in their own right but raised the bar for me every day. We also shared a pack mentality. The gang ethos I had grown up with in Manchester prevailed within our training group: we lifted one another, protected one another and supported one another. Jamie was the sharp-witted character within the group who was unafraid to call things out, to everyone's benefit. Honesty and transparency enabled us to squeeze every last inch of talent out of ourselves. We all recognised this, and behaved in a manner that benefitted us all. Should any of us show up for training not quite up to the mark, other members of the group would always brutally expose those failings through ruthless banter, and by stepping up their own efforts on the track to reveal the gap in performance that had now been created. The ruthlessness was relentless. I can recall several sessions where I would be left in the dust by my two colleagues until I was sharp enough, which sometimes made the level of competition within our group as high as elite level events. With Jamie and Paul as track partners the jump from training to competing was small.

This carried over into other aspects of our lives. We protected one another, and celebrated with one another. When I won gold, my first title, at the European Championships in Budapest, I was chased down and mobbed by Paul and Jamie almost as if they had won the medal themselves. They felt as much of my success as I did, which they were absolutely entitled to and I took delight in. I felt equally proud of Paul's Commonwealth medals and Jamie's collection of World, European and Commonwealth successes.

Athletics could, and I'm sure still can, be a sport where individuals feel like they take on the world themselves. This can lead to some backbiting and intimidation of shrinking violets in the quest for competitive advantage. It is probably an understatement to suggest that there was safety in being part of the Baulch, Campbell, Gray clan, and there would have been no question of anyone having the temerity to attempt to undermine or intimidate a group that took pride in looking after one another's backs with vigour.

Finishing my career made me reflect on my own achievements and experiences with great nostalgia. In the moments before falling asleep each night I remained thankful that I had been blessed, and was able to recall key life-moments such as lining up for an Olympic 100m final, or being taken through the war-torn neighbourhoods of Sarajevo, or being given a second chance at family life. I became more philosophical about my own achievements. The 15-year-old Darren would be beside himself with joy at the prospect of becoming a future Olympic gold medallist, yet 30-year-old Darren took more pleasure from the radiance of his children's faces than the shine of that same medal. Priorities and feelings had changed.

One of the more pleasant aspects of life became a post-training ritual with my children. I would often return from training absolutely exhausted and collapse asleep on the sofa at home. Aaryn and Dillan as young children would climb on top of me, resting their heads on my chest and legs, and join their dad in a power nap. When that experience became as much of a reason to train as training itself, I knew things were winding down.

It was with this adjustment in outlook, combined with a body that was breaking down more often and needed a longer and longer recovery time, which made retirement easy. I was lucky, in a sense, that I had achieved my life goals by the time reality dawned on me. I retired at my own time on my own terms. I can sympathise wholeheartedly with sports people who have to deal with the frustration of injury curtailing their careers, or having to suffer the hurt of not reaching the levels their talents justified. The chasm that awaits afterwards can be a deep one. I was never the type to make a comeback for 'one last race' in order to prove something – I was content being content with my achievements.

RETIREMENT

In a similar vein to *needing* to achieve high goals in athletics, maybe because of my own personal history, I *needed* to be a good father over all else. I wanted to be a person that my children could come to with anything, and be regarded by them as someone who didn't hide the realities of life away from them. I always tried to be as close to my children as possible, from hugging them while watching television to being with them as often as I could, even if it meant being away from the work I needed to do in order to be able to make a living. My job as an athlete had forced me to be more selfish than a normal person, and required me to reduce the weight that life could impose upon me: I needed to be 'responsibility-light'. As my friend Lynx would say, I would often "go ghost" at certain points in my career, by removing myself from the family in order to totally focus on improving my performance. Now that athletics was winding down, I wanted my children to see their dad, not as a ghost-like figure – elusive and rarely seen – but to be a physically present constant in their lives.

My newly-found 'spare' time also allowed me to explore new projects, such as the Team Super Schools initiative I set up with Linford. I really enjoyed getting involved with numerous worthy initiatives through which I was able to widen my horizons, apply my skills and experience, and inject my passion and enthusiasm.

11

Coach

"No! The first one she's going to wear is the one she wins!"
Julie Asher-Smith

I first met Jon Williams around the start of the millennium when I was still involved in athletics. I had called into a local health food store, looking for a tub of protein and some multivitamins. Standing in that same aisle at the same time was Jon. He was an up-and-coming figure in the world of nutrition and as we got to know each other he became one of those people whose opinions I trusted and respected. In his day he had been a more than average bodybuilder – another sport synonymous with self-discipline and hard work. It was also, like athletics, a sport regularly tainted with the nefarious behaviours of cheats and drug abusers, and although these are probably in the minority, to the outside world it seems that everyone is tainted with the same brush.

Thanks to his thirst for knowledge and understanding of the body's nutritional needs, Jon was a pioneer. He was one of those people whose values of fair play and strict discipline echoed my own. Having decided to abandon my career in athletics – partly due to a desire to adopt the moral high ground and keep a clean sheet in the drugs department – meeting Jon was a godsend. I badly needed his advice at a time when I was surrounded by people trying desperately to have me return to the track. However, by now, I had become disillusioned and frustrated at the fraudulent success of others. Meeting Jon was a meeting of minds, values and needs; we got on as individuals and 25 years later we are still good friends.

COACH

Jon advised me of the concepts of periodising nutrition in the same way that coaches periodised training. He enhanced my knowledge and elevated my way of thinking when it came to food, and also in the, still fledgling, theories of sports supplementation. Athletes were aware of the benefits of correct eating while training, as well as certain protein and creatine supplementation. However, the level of ignorance was high enough throughout society as a whole that it was perceived that supplementation was close enough to the concept of 'artificial' doping for it to be treated with suspicion. We immediately saw where our principles of clean sport and heightened nutritional knowledge would align. We noticed that in the confusing world of supplementation, where even products sold by known brands weren't always aligned with the most up-to-date doping list, we could sell a concept: trust. We were of course selling a product, but the biggest thing we were selling – from athletes to athletes – was peace of mind.

We established Pro Athlete Supplementation, known as PAS Nutrition, to be at the forefront of sports nutrition, not only from a performance standpoint, but also from the platform of integrity. Frustratingly, we found that creating the former was easy, whereas ensuring the latter was jaw-droppingly costly.

Testing supplements for cleanliness, lack of cross-contamination and purity, was very costly at the start and ate so far into our profit margins that we began to question the sanity of the entire business model. To be accredited with what was to become the globally trusted – yet, to this day, still not compulsory – Informed Sport logo, cost us thousands upon thousands of pounds. I found that – as with my career in athletics – our profit margins would have been greater had we been a lot less honest and principled. For the first few years of the business, we couldn't even take a salary.

Jon had developed a strong understanding of the body's nutritional needs through his own experiences, and was committed to developing a deeper knowledge and wider experience of the science. This was at a time when society was waking up to the benefits of diet on high performance sport. His advice helped me immensely as an athlete and I felt energised that committing more to the sports nutrition company would help ease me through the transition from full-time athletics to retirement. Jon, and many of his mentees, have since become nutritional advisors to many professional football teams and international rugby teams including the Grand Slam-winning Wales national rugby team and Premier League winners Leicester City. My gut feeling that this guy was a cut above the rest served me well and proved correct several times over.

It became hard to distinguish between close friends and colleagues at PAS, such was the camaraderie within the company. Kevin Walker and Gary Walters, both former sportsmen, applied the dedication, loyalty, work-rate and conscientiousness they developed through sport to help us make the company stronger and well-respected. We would not have had the success – or indeed the good name we generated – without them. On a personal level, having strong people I can trust around me has been as important for my involvement with PAS as it had been throughout my entire athletics career.

An interesting by-product of aligning myself with PAS was that I crossed paths with a much larger number of sports, coaches and athletes. My profile as a gold medal-winning Olympian certainly helped enhance the credibility of our business, and when we were in key meetings the conversations alternated between discussions regarding nutrition with Jon and training methods with me.

One example of this was with the Cardiff Blues rugby union team. The team had been successful for a brief period, winning various titles – including a soon-to-be European Challenge Cup trophy – as well as figuring well in their league competition. A large proportion of the squad were not only talented players but – by chance, design and recruitment – exceptionally quick. The team had also signed Jonah Lomu who, at the time, was not only the biggest name in the rugby world but was also one of the most famous people on the planet. Jonah had got in touch with me through his agent as he had heard that I was living in south Wales, and we became friends. His motivation in signing for Cardiff was to re-ignite his career that had been sadly affected by kidney failure, which was tragically to prove fatal in 2015.

Jonah had scored some of the most famous tries in the history of the sport, and at his peak was capable of running sub 11 seconds for the 100m while weighing in at over 110kg. He felt that his speed had become an area to work on during his enforced time away while recuperating, so we exchanged phone numbers, met for coffee a few times, and discussed ways of helping him. During our chats, Jonah shared with me his love of cars, music, and also for track and field athletics. Our experience of life was also similar in that he had experienced difficulties growing up in South Auckland. As a young man he had been involved in fights, drank too much and was known to the Auckland police as a troublemaker. He found his escape through rugby, in the same way that I had through athletics. Pointedly, his relationship with his father had been fractious and sometime aggressive. We had a lot in common, although I'd never had the opportunity of being able to fall out and argue with my father. Our parallel backgrounds made it almost inevitable that we would have a lot to discuss even before the conversation turned to sport and training.

Jonah, being the consummate professional, and frankly the very nice guy he was, didn't want to upset the apple cart at his new club. Coaches employed by teams could be notoriously prickly and even territorial when it came to external training influences on their squad players. Since Jonah's arrival at Cardiff had been plastered all over the media weeks before his arrival, the potential for new entourages to form around him was great and this threat needed a Jonah-style fend off from the club's point of view. He was here to play rugby, to re-boot his career, and the number of distractions needed to be minimised. Having been there myself years earlier, I knew first-hand the danger of allowing distractions and hangers-on to cloud the task at hand. I thought I could help and wanted to be useful if I could. That was my only agenda.

Luckily, it transpired that a coach at Cardiff had a relatively decent track and field background himself and had represented Wales at the 400m hurdles. He felt that having an Olympic champion's expertise and experience nearby could be the key to unlocking further successes. Coincidentally, he had been purposefully elevating speed further up the training agenda within the club for a few seasons, and had no issue with me working with Jonah. His boss, the coach David 'Dai' Young who not only had enjoyed his own stellar career as a player but then went on to further success coaching the Cardiff Blues, and Wasps, managed to get signed-off what was, at the time, a remarkably far-sighted and rare appointment in professional rugby union – I was asked to become a speed coach at the Cardiff Blues. I'd inadvertently got a lot more than I had bargained for. I'd agreed to help Jonah, and ended up coaching the entire squad.

The players that the coaches at Cardiff identified as being 'rather quick' included youngsters such as Leigh Halfpenny from Gorseinon near Swansea, a player bizarrely deemed surplus to requirements at his local team the Ospreys. His physical and technical qualities were so superlative as to make a mockery of the Ospreys' decision even before he became well-known. Leigh went on to be one of the most celebrated players in the world, whose kicking accuracy was so precise he'd put a laser to shame. Yet what struck me was his devastating speed. From early on in his career he scored length-of-the-field tries for Cardiff and Wales, ghosting past defenders with devastating ease. Over time, however, his role in the team became that of a kicker and catcher in the backfield, almost like a defensive sweeper in football. This meant that this razor-sharp sprinter was now being used as more of a middle-distance runner, but it was testament to his ability that he could adapt so well and thrive.

There was also this tall muscular figure, Sam Warburton, a former pupil at Whitchurch High School in Cardiff, which also produced footballer Gareth Bale and cyclist Geraint Thomas. An openside flanker with a sharp acceleration and immense power within his lean frame, Sam was the obvious contender to replace the 100-times capped Martyn Williams' in the number seven jersey at the Blues. Not only did he make a huge success of that, Sam eventually captained Wales and the British Lions before injury forced him into an early retirement.

Less than a mile from Whitchurch High was another Cardiff sporting hotbed, the Welsh-language high school Ysgol Glantaf, from where the large imposing figure of a young starlet called Jamie Roberts burst into the Blues squad. He was a fullback/wing prior to becoming a barnstorming centre for Wales and the Lions. During the limited time I spent with Jamie, before he was inevitably whisked away for national duty, I found him to be one of the most studious sportspeople I had ever met and it was no surprise that he took a medical degree alongside playing professional rugby and became a fully qualified doctor. Having conversations over gait and its effect on anatomy with a young rugby player whilst walking back to the changing room from the track was certainly not something I expected when I began coaching.

These soon-to-be household names also benefited from having stars from the southern hemisphere join the club who played a part in developing and maintaining phenomenally high standards of training and preparation. It made my job as a coach relatively easy, and my first experience of the world of team sports left me with the impression that the gap in discipline, standards and professionalism wasn't as large as many of those in the individual sports world would have us believe.

Athletes used to – and maybe still do – have a slightly superior attitude when it comes to the diligence and standards of training in individual sports compared with team sports. Despite the differences being obvious, elite rugby certainly compared favourably when it came to training standards. Don't misinterpret my compliments – players' fitness was a million miles away from an elite cyclist or marathon runner and their speed was nowhere near that of an elite sprinter – but their ability to have plentiful reserves of strength, speed, fitness and power was impressive. One of the Blues' players I've mentioned was easily able to squat twice his body weight, run 100m in circa 11 seconds while at the same time cover the equivalent of five miles in a game of rugby. To those training aficionados who may be interested, there was a young starlet called Josh Navidi – a future Wales international – who could 'power clean' close to 150kg. These are elite level performances in any sport.

In time, the sporting contacts grew exponentially and being a coach became a viable option for me to pursue as a parallel career. The supplements business was always going to take precedence but when I received phone calls from rugby players such as England winger Mark Cueto and his fellow international, scrum-half Richard Wigglesworth, and when Bryan English – at this point involved with Chelsea – asked me to help out with Ukrainian football star Andriy Shevchenko my coaching consultancy took on its own momentum. More importantly, I enjoyed it. The transition from being a full-time sportsman had been hard for many of my colleagues, but the fact that I could leave the track as an athlete, yet slowly return to the track as a coach, eased the experience for me. It made retiring from sport a gentler proposition. Retirement from sport and its link to mental health is finally getting the attention it deserves, because the change is truly monumental.

Brought to the club by José Mourinho, 'Sheva' was going through a rough patch as a Chelsea player, with his huge transfer fee of £31 million putting a lot of pressure on him to succeed. This, coupled with an ever-increasing list of injuries made him a target for both board members and fans of the club alike. Avram Grant, who succeeded Mourinho at Stamford Bridge, welcomed any support that I could offer Andriy, and the player himself was desperate to recover and keen to learn. The main areas of concern related to soft tissue injuries, and running at high speed was a problem. In the quest to resolve this, he was inadvertently aggravating the niggles that were causing him those problems in the first place.

The backroom staff at Chelsea, to their credit, made me feel very welcome and in time I was invited to help out with more squad players including Nicolas Anelka and Didier Drogba. This was when I first met future Swansea, Liverpool, Celtic and Leicester City manager, Brendan Rodgers, who was part of the Chelsea backroom staff. He was always very inquisitive and showed a passion and interest in what I was doing that was way beyond the standard thinking of coaches.

I didn't try to make Shevchenko run like an Olympic sprinter, or change his running gait biomechanically. That would have been futile for an athlete who was already at the peak of his physical power, in a sport which requires many forms of running. We decided to concentrate on his reactiveness and acceleration, and when dealing with such a high profile and expensive player, I felt I had to err on the side of caution: a lesson in asset management that all sports coaches in most team sports would be familiar with.

A few years later I had an interesting conversation with a coach from a rival team – a team whose players had a net worth of close to half a billion pounds. I asked him, "What protocols do you have in place to minimise injuries during high speed training sessions?" His answer was a broad smile and a pose which indicated he was looking to the sky as if in prayer!! The lesson being that you could minimise the risk, but never guarantee anything, and to pretend otherwise either was slightly naïve or making undeliverable promises.

Due to the combined efforts of all the backroom staff at Chelsea, things improved significantly for Shevchenko. His goal tally increased in the second half of the season and he won more than one man-of-the-match award but, such is the life of a sports person – both coach and player – that when Luis Felipe Scolari assumed the manager's mantle at Stamford Bridge, Sheva was soon on a plane heading back to AC Milan.

After my time with Chelsea I found work closer to home with Cardiff City Football Club, and started taking the occasional session with Saracens Rugby. I was part of Cardiff City's attached backroom as they were promoted to the Premier League with manager Malky Mackay at the helm, and it was a welcome return to an old stomping ground for me as they shared a training base with the Cardiff Blues. The Bluebirds secured an unlikely promotion – winning the Championship Trophy in the process – but there was a general feeling that the team was far greater than the sum of its parts and that it would struggle with the much higher standards of the Premier League.

Cardiff had significant quality within their ranks – with players such as French striker Rudy Gestede, Chilean star Gary Medel, the late Peter Whittingham and Welsh legend Craig Bellamy – but they had undoubtedly managed to beat all the odds, and significantly stronger playing squads, to achieve Premier League status. This was due in no small part to the superhuman effort put in, week-in week-out, by their star players, something which would be unsustainable in the Premier League when every single game would be a 'cup final'.

During my time at Cardiff City that season, player development was, of necessity, confined to the back burner as there was no time to work on speed or sharpen reactions. The timetable for the week read like this: training, playing, resting, training. To be honest, with so many millions of pounds resting on the team's success, it was hard to argue with that rationale. Cardiff held their own in the opening months of their Premier League campaign but the wheels came off when friction between the manager and the owner led to Malky being sacked and the team struggled from then on. I was lucky enough to have the opportunity to work under one of my Manchester United heroes, Ole Gunnar Solsjkær, who had replaced Malky, but even he couldn't save the Bluebirds from relegation.

At this time my company, PAS, was gaining significant traction as official nutritional suppliers to many international and club teams in both football and rugby. Under the leadership of Warren Gatland Welsh rugby was experiencing a golden era, and the squad not only used the PAS supplements, but also benefitted from Jon Williams' expertise and knowledge which was incorporated in their training programme. There were some significant individual successes too with Leigh Halfpenny and Sam Warburton proving to be wonderful advocates for our programme: their 'before and after' photo shoots showed Leigh sporting his new bulging biceps whilst Sam was now a 'vein-throbbing hulk'.

The next invitation meant crossing Offa's Dyke and spending Tuesday mornings with Wasps Rugby in the West Midlands. They had recently relocated from their west London base in Acton and were now playing their games at the magnificent Ricoh Arena on the outskirts of Coventry. Wasps had within their ranks the likes of outrageous Australian superstar Kurtley Beale, World Cup winning Springbok Willie Le Roux, and the talented English trio of Elliot Daly, Danny Cipriani and Christian Wade.

Wasps had become both notorious and famous for a high-risk and phenomenally entertaining brand of rugby, and being able to help with their speedwork was truly a pleasure. Despite being labelled by many sections of the press as maverick, chancy and individualistic in their play, I must say that their approach to training with me was industrious and conscientious. Wade especially – who was to move to the NFL a few years later – was a complete one-off insomuch that he was exceptionally sharp and agile, both physically and mentally, but enjoyed assuming the persona of being laid-back and carefree. Wade was a decent sprinter in his youth – around 10.8 seconds for the 100m – and had been coached by my good friend Julian Golding, which meant in rugby terms he was simply untouchable. Cipriani, who was playing some of the most spellbinding rugby of his career, I found to be attentive and interested in everything I had to offer and keen to improve his acceleration. Elliot Daly was the proverbial buzzing bee, never stopping for a second and racing everyone and everything in sight. He had the unbounded energy akin to a world-class middle-distance runner.

This group reminded me of the gang mentality that I had grown up with in and around Moss Side. The Wasps players seemed to enjoy each other's company immensely, feeding off one another, and once training was over they were in no hurry to leave the training base. Apparently, the team coach once stopped at a motorway service station on the M5 where, by coincidence, there was another coach full of Wasps fans in the same car park. What followed was an impromptu game of cricket, with British Lion Elliot Daly showcasing his right arm over-the-wicket bowling action to a lifelong Wasps supporter, with Kurtley Beale, Joe Launchbury and Dan Robson in close attendance as slip fielders. It is true to say that those fans probably dined on this experience for weeks to come. I always drove away from the Coventry training base with a smile on my face.

The next drive however was a little longer, as it took me to Middlesborough Football Club to work under manager Tony Pulis.

COACH

Bryan English, the British team doctor from my athletics career, had moved on to work at Middlesborough having left athletics to work in other sports, serving organisations such as Chelsea FC and the Lawn Tennis Association with distinction. Bryan's approach to speed training was sophisticated, correlating it with bullet-proofing players with regard to injury prevention as well as improving performance. Middlesborough during this time had some talented athletes on its books including the Frenchman I had previously worked with at Cardiff, Rudy Gestede, who went on to play international football for Benin. Rudy was a tremendously talented athlete whose long legs and wide running gait made him an asset for chasing long balls, but mechanically disadvantaged when it came to turning and accelerating. Rudy and I had worked at Cardiff and got along, and while at Middlesborough he bought into Bryan's concepts of working on speed – as a form of injury rehabilitation – with great passion, and after fracturing his ankle in February of that season he returned to play in May, an astonishingly quick recovery for a footballer.

During my first trip up to Middlesborough, I was sitting in the training ground restaurant with Rudy and a few other players when Adama Traoré came to join us. After a brief conversation, I mentioned to him, "You have no idea how good you could be and how I could help you". It was a confident statement, but we both laughed and he agreed to let me assist him. I taught him how to control his speed and, through training, encouraged his ability to run with more efficiency with the ball at his feet. He later signed for Wolves for £18 million.

I feel honoured to have played a very small part in supporting a number of talented sportsmen, as well as those who take part simply for enjoyment. The concept of 'giving something back' has become a well-worn cliché – as well as a newly-adopted form of humble-bragging since the growth of social media – yet since leaving athletics I have found I have an instinctive urge to help, which simply won't leave me. In the same way that Aaryn, Dillan and Leoni grind their teeth in frustration and ultimately have a reflex action to help when Clair and I are struggling with our iPads or with technology, I have an impulse to share my thoughts, based on my many mistakes and a few successes, to others who are on their own sporting journeys. If people listen, it is a privilege for me. A part of gaining experience involves making our own mistakes and working through difficult times, but I actively enjoy informing others of the perils and the opportunities that sport presents.

In 2008 I had co-founded the Team Superschools project with Todd Bennett, one of Britain's most successful 400m runners and who tragically lost his battle with cancer in 2013. I remember the fateful phone call I had with Todd where I could sense that there was something not quite right in his huskier-than-usual voice. I joked that I could send him some nutrition and vitamins from my company's product range to help his health. He replied very matter-of-factly, and with extraordinary dignity, that his body was riddled with cancer and it was a little more serious than a common cold. Todd knew that he was going to die, and he decided that he wanted to plan his legacy through the Team Superschools project so that it would continue after he passed away. Todd Bennett was a kind benevolent man, and he even suggested that we find someone to carry on his work for the project. We both agreed that Jason Gardener was the perfect person. His values and nature mirrored Todd's and would ensure that the essence of the project would continue.

Todd's passing taught me that there could be dignity in death. I spoke at Todd's funeral which was a huge privilege because Todd Bennett was looked upon as one of British sport's genuinely good people. I had promised myself, in a prayer, that if life bestowed on me the blessing of an Olympic gold medal, I would use that for whatever good I could, maybe even to inspire others. Team Superschools was one of the vehicles I used to repay that promise.

When we started Team Superschools in 2008 it was, and still is, an initiative designed to support and promote sport in schools. The plan was to visit 2,012 schools before the London 2012 Olympics, bringing sporting ambassadors and school pupils together, and we were also able to bring in athletes from our past such as the Commonwealth 400m gold medal winner, Adrian Patrick, and Amy Williams, the winter Olympic champion, to help deliver the Team Superschools message.

We travelled widely, spoke at teachers' conferences, attended school inset days and built the project around the central focus of engagement with schools. We also decided that any money raised would be used to provide bursaries and grants. One day we went to Newstead Wood School in Orpington, south east London, where I met Dina, a young enthusiastic runner with a beaming smile. We had a photo taken together, in which she held my Athens Olympic gold medal, but upon asking if she wanted to wear it, Julie, her mum, interjected with a firm: "No! The first one she's going to wear is the one she wins!"

I loved that attitude and even then I could see that the right combination of humour and seriousness was evident. I had experienced a similar attitude in never wanting to see my coach Linford Christie's Olympic gold medal, for the very same reason, so Julie's comment struck a chord with me. Team Superschools awarded Dina one of our first ever grants. It was an inspired choice, for the lady who had called Todd Bennett enquiring about the scheme, and who was determined *not* for her daughter to wear an Olympic gold medal until she had one of her own was Julie Asher-Smith. In less than a decade, her daughter Dina Asher-Smith would have many medals of her own and would be inspiring a new generation of athletes.

In an interview we did together on BBC Radio 5Live in 2018, when Dina was a multiple gold medal winner from the European Championships, we reminisced over how we had met for the first time and how our paths had crossed over the years. During this conversation it became apparent that current day athletes inspiring the next generation was a strong part of Dina's own personal story. As fate would have it, Dina was a 'box carrier' for the London 2012 Olympic Games. Box carriers, similar to ball boys and girls at Wimbledon, were selected from local schools around London and trained to perform duties close to where the action happened. It is fantastic to consider that Dina Asher-Smith was a teenager, on the track, carrying equipment and athletes' kits just outside lane eight on the famous 'Super Saturday' when Greg Rutherford, Jessica Ennis and Mo Farah won their gold medals. Fast forward six years, and World 200m champion Dina would be calling them "Greg, Jess and Mo": inspiration indeed. Dina, being the kind-hearted angel that she is, was also one of the first people to reach out to me when I suffered my illness.

During this period, I also became an ambassador for the Youth Sports Trust charity, as well as the Living for Sport initiative launched by Sky Sports, alongside such luminaries as David Beckham and Jessica Ennis-Hill. Being able to interact with leading figures from other sports to inspire the next generation was incredibly rewarding, and I was invited to speak at various events, including those arranged by political parties. Despite being relatively non party political, I felt it was important to interact with all opinion formers and decision makers in the hope that such networking might benefit others. I remember addressing the Liberal Democrats and the Labour Party, primarily speaking about my own career and background, but also attempting to gain traction and profile for the trusts and initiatives that I had become involved in.

I met Jo Osbourne through the programme *Game Changers*. She was involved in developing a new kids television show in conjunction with the Living for Sport initiative. She had a big picture holistic view of the whole situation, and through *Game Changers* tried to build a really inclusive positive show that everyone enjoyed watching. I was recommended as a potential presenter to her, and we hit it off immediately. The show was fun since it was live, but this also made it daunting for me as someone new to that role. I had not presented before, and needed to slowly and gently ease myself into doing it.

The initial plan was that my co-presenter Di Docherty would read the autocue and I would just chip in, but due to Jo's confidence in my ability the plan lasted for maybe a week before the chemistry and spontaneity of the show took over. Reading an autocue was initially a problem for me, but the essence of the show was instructing children to enjoy and overcome their fears so, when the lights came on, I couldn't tell the audience they have to overcome fear if I didn't attempt to do that myself. Filmed in Studio F, in the Sky TV complex in Isleworth, where *Soccer AM* is recorded, the show was very ambitious and it was fun for the kids. Our aim of having a good time shone through the screen to the audience and it became a good opportunity to create something to be really proud of.

We had some fun experiences on the show, such as when we welcomed two rugby players from Bath RFC and, naturally, the show's producers (naming no names – Jo Osbourne) decided to put me in a bath: Olly Murs was placed in one of those huge see-through bouncing zorb footballs, so I feel I got off lightly. Prince Harry and David Beckham came on the show and we also had Dina Asher-Smith guest-presenting. The off-the-cuff chemistry, combined with a lot of love and care, made the show's organised spontaneity infectious. The small team punched above its weight and, to this day, it is one of the things I'm most proud of.

I learnt that even in a high-octane live environment, people with the same attitude and same positivity can yield special things. *Game Changers* was such a fulfilling thing to work on, particularly since we built a whole show from scratch every week. We created props, sets, scenes, and worked exceptionally hard to make it inclusive. The whole ethos was a 'do it at home with your parents – no equipment needed' feel, and it made sport and fitness accessible to a wide audience.

Two individuals who believed in my ability to hold an audience from behind a microphone were Mike Carr, the former editor of BBC Radio Sport and 5Live, and the BBC's boxing and athletics correspondent Mike Costello, and thanks to Mike I was approached by the BBC to do little bits and bobs on the radio. At this time, former Arsenal and England footballing legend Ian Wright was doing really well with his own career on the BBC both as a presenter and pundit, so I called him to ask his advice. Ian explained that from his own experiences, the BBC was fantastic as far as teaching the skills necessary to progress. He also felt he was being well looked after and treated with great respect by its staff.

The BBC offer was an attractive one, because they had the contract to broadcast the Olympic Games. This was an event that meant a great deal to me and the opportunity to be a part of it, in any shape or form, would be too good to turn down. Mike Carr was exceptionally good at his job and was aware of my strengths and weaknesses. At the BBC there is a template of 'how to be' but there is also freedom to be yourself. Mike put me in a situation where my broadcasting skills were not unduly challenged but he also encouraged me to expand my repertoire, saying I would improve with experience. An example of this was how he taught me to repeat a sentence, with a smile on my face. This would alter the tone of my voice and improve communications with the listeners. These little tricks and broadcasting wisdom made a world of difference, and were very useful when broadcasting with Alan Brazil on Talksport.

If I ever find myself commentating on Dina Asher-Smith winning an Olympic medal, it is fair to say I will not need to put a smile on my face. Maybe then Julie will allow us to briefly wear each other's medals for a photograph!

Epilogue

The Toughest Race of My Life

'A pituitary apoplexy occurs suddenly. Symptoms are caused by a build-up of pressure in the space surrounding the pituitary gland. It is life-threatening and requires urgent medical diagnosis. Symptoms include severe, sudden-onset headache, nausea and vomiting, paralysis, affecting visual impairment and decreased consciousness.'

We are always afraid of the things we cannot control or understand. We all also believe that we are indestructible – right up to the point that something happens to remind us we're not.

Many fit and healthy sport stars have suffered exceptional and unexpected medical issues, either during their careers or sometimes as long as a decade or so after their physical peak. They include Gareth Thomas, the Wales dual-code rugby international. He suffered a stroke while still a professional player and, physically speaking, in the shape of his life. Tedy Bruschi, a linebacker for the New England Patriots, suffered a stroke just days after playing in an NFL Pro Bowl game. Fitness and athletic ability has no correlation to health when it comes to the brain and I never thought that I would join that illustrious list. Describing what it feels like is almost impossible, as it was an outer-body and outer-mind experience. The one thing that I can remember, however, is the initial fear when it struck.

We all suffer from headaches. Anyone who drives a car regularly or works in front of a computer screen all day can empathise with the sensation of suffering from headaches, and fatigue of the eyes and the neck muscles. I had suffered with this for years on the long car drives to and from Manchester, where taking breaks meant a few minutes respite before a few more hours sat behind the wheel, staring at oncoming bright headlights through driving rain.

The pituitary apoplexy, however, came from nowhere. The circumstances surrounding it are patchy, and I cannot be entirely certain of the timeline and what came first. I know I had a brain bleed while sleeping, but I also remember periods of intense conscious pain while being wide awake. There was a constant acute pain just beneath my skull at the juncture with the neck muscles, and in attempting to relax and control my breathing to counteract the rapidly elevated pain levels, I could feel a strange sensation accompanying the headache: a stiffening of muscles around the neck, and a rigidity going up into the back of my skull which triggered a pounding headache. I know I must have blacked out many times. I became a frightened, aggressive, upset, confused person and the truly petrifying thing about the whole event was that it happened so quickly. The pain was indescribable, but so was the fear. I assumed that I may have seen my wife and children for the last time.

The irony of the incident was the timing; that it happened when it did. If I was predisposed to such a thing, and if stress was a trigger, it should have happened years previously. I had dealt with stresses and flashpoints before: while being apart from Clair, coping with the tensions and expectations of being an athlete, during the early days of the PAS business, or in my younger days carving out a life on the streets of Sale Racecourse. At any point during those periods I would have been in a position, psychologically, to trigger some kind of stress-related illness. When it struck, I was an early 40s, relatively fit and healthy individual with no immediate worries and whose business was thriving. There were no anxieties over and above the usual ones that cross the desk of any husband and father with three children and a mortgage to pay.

I still don't know what caused it, but the scariest aspect was the fact that I had no idea how to control its legacy and effects. I also cannot remember anything at all after the incident. My hunch was that pent-up emotions might have come out in one explosion of pressure. It scared me more thinking that there might not have been a direct cause.

I was rushed to Royal Gwent Hospital in Newport and immediately placed in the intensive care ward. My friends, including Lynx, rushed down all the way from Manchester to be at my side and to support Clair and the children. Lynx joked with me, in time, that he thought it was so serious that they didn't even stop for a McDonald's at the motorway services on the way. Even in times of life and death, the Mancunian humour was never far from the surface.

Upon their arrival, the sight that welcomed my friends and family at the hospital was of tubes, ventilators and beeping machines surrounding a motionless body wearing a mask. They were told that I had nearly died, twice, but that I had stabilised and the phenomenal staff at the Royal Gwent were now taking care of me. I was unaware of the entire experience as I was unconscious and on the verge of slipping into a coma. A week after the initial apoplexy, I suffered a relapse which resulted in my being placed on life-support for a brief period. I cannot imagine the pain and anxiety that Clair, Aaryn, Dillan and Leoni suffered. They were strong in the moment because they are resilient and mature people, but having to cope with this was something my family did not deserve.

When I opened my eyes and saw my family and friends, it was unreal. I had no idea where I was. I had no memory of what had happened, and I had very little comprehension of what was going on. I was absolutely certain that I was still in a dream, and that this madness would resolve itself as soon as I woke up. Whether it was the effect of the multitude of painkilling drugs or the dreamy surrealness of it all, I merely slipped in and out of sleep convinced that this was not reality.

The brain injury stripped me of everything I ever had. My physical attributes as an athlete had given me the ability to earn a living, but this was now completely destroyed. I was reduced to being a body with no capability and being helped to breathe. The ambition I had as an athlete and a businessman also became completely irrelevant in face of the apoplexy. Everything I had established – friendships, family, business, wealth, respect, career – all fell on the sword of simply being able to breathe one breath after another. Yet little did I know that the toughest journey was about to come. I needed something to take the blame for such a momentous event. There had to be a reason why it happened, and for me to make the appropriate adjustment for it to never happen again, but the fact that there was no direct cause was very confusing and a little disturbing. To be devoid of a cause meant I didn't have the closure of knowing an episode had come and gone in my life from which I had learnt and adapted to. It wasn't so much for

EPILOGUE

my own peace of mind, but for my family's. The faith that we all have in surgeons and doctors is a wonderful thing and entirely deserved, but the human body is the most complex machine ever created, with billions of chemical, biological and anatomical variables working together, so to be faced with an unsure answer to such a serious question left me unfulfilled and worried.

NHS staff are the most fantastic, skilled and compassionate people. Maybe because of which, they are undervalued and taken for granted like a benevolent grandmother or guardian angel who'll always be there for us. I owe my life to the staff at Newport's Royal Gwent and the thanks that I give them can only be measured in how I treat my children, family and friends in the days months and years that I now have with them because of the NHS' intervention.

The physical recovery was relatively quick. I was up on my feet walking – very slowly – within days, but everything from then on was slow and tiresome. Despite being fatigued and low on energy and vitality, sleeping became a chore. Who wants to go to bed when all you have done for a month is stay in bed? I was caught in the bizarre situation of having a renewed appreciation for everything that was around me but lacking the energy to appreciate it. My own humour enabled me to feel supremely blessed for merely still being here, to be able to moan about how everything hurt and how I couldn't do half the things I wanted to do.

I conducted an interview with the *Daily Mail* a few months into my recovery, a process which I found surprisingly cathartic. The sports writer, Riath Al-Samarrai, came to our home and I found the experience of attempting to recount my experience, as well as convey to him as eloquently as I could how the experience had been emotionally cleansing. He was wonderfully empathetic and sympathetic in equal measure, knowing that this was the first time I had attempted anything resembling a deep dive back into that dark hole. Having attempted to rationalise everything in my own head for months – and failing to do so – answering questions from a journalist seemed a simpler, safer and more structured way of revisiting my personal horror.

What was staggering was the love and support that I received from friends, peers and colleagues over the next few months. I received countless texts and phone calls, house visits – which I'm sure drove Clair mad as she was completely determined to keep me relaxed and undisturbed – and messages on social media from complete strangers who had reached out to wish me well. I had got to know, and coach, the French Congolese footballer Yannick Bolasie when he played for Everton and we struck up a close friendship. After hearing of my experience, Yannick paid for my family and me to go and recuperate in Portugal. An act of such kindness that had a huge impact on me. It also meant a lot because I felt Clair and the kids needed a breather as much as I did. Such benevolent, kind friends are worth their weight in gold.

The experience of coming so close to losing everything made me realise what I had. It also reminded me of a very similar experience, and a similar emotion, I had felt three decades earlier. When I was ten years old, Mum had taken me back to Hanover in Jamaica to see where, and more importantly how, she had grown up. Mum was born on the west coast of Jamaica, and lived there until 1962 when she moved to the United Kingdom. This was the time when Jamaican residents lived through the Cuban Missile Crisis taking place a mere 100 or so miles away across the Cayman trench, and when they saw the rise of the Haitian cult leader and voodoo priest Papa Doc Duvalier some 200 miles across the Jamaica Channel to the east. Also around this time, about 80 miles to the east of Hanover in Nine Mile, a young Robert Nesta Marley was playing with his band The Teenagers; who would ultimately change their name to The Wailers. One could easily press a case that early 1960s Jamaica was ideologically, musically and politically, close to being the epicentre of the world for a brief period. It must have been a frightening yet exhilarating place to exist. Yet for Mum, it was also a tough place. There was very little economic prosperity, and the opportunities for social progression were almost nil.

The family came from the 'bush' area of Hanover. A mountainous area, rooted in a history of sugar plantations and slavery, Hanover is Jamaica's smallest region. The family home was a meagre and humble house set within deep hills and surrounded by countryside, where locals would pick their own food and live a very humble life indeed. I stayed there for three months, living as a local. It was a complete departure from what I knew. Picking my own food and calling the baking hot dusty roads and old plantations 'home' was surreal.

EPILOGUE

When I returned to Manchester, our house in Sale had been robbed. Despite this, it was good to be home. I had absolutely loved my time in Jamaica, but the message that Mum had intended for me to absorb was received loud and clear. We were lucky to have what we had in Manchester. Things were better for us there than back in Jamaica, despite the obvious challenges and threats. I felt as lucky and thankful in returning to Sale as I felt recovering from my brain bleed in Newport's Royal Gwent Hospital.

A lifetime in sport had enabled me to compartmentalise, to block out distractions, to plan, strategise and to take control of all variables that could potentially come my way. A background of growing up in a tough area gave me an appreciation of how lucky and blessed I had become in achieving my goals in sport. Being a father and husband to a wonderful family gave me a purpose with which to look forward and to ensure each new day could bring further happiness.

In nearly dying, the pituitary apoplexy taught me one very important lesson: all the troubles and efforts that had come my way previously had toughened me, made me more resilient and more able to take on unexpected challenges. I wouldn't have come through the brain bleed had I not had the strength to come through the rest of my life, of that I have no doubt.

Had my personal track record been one of a life catalogued by transgressions and regressive behaviour, I doubt I would have had the physical or mental strength to recover. I believe I survived and flourished because of my drive and determination, my desire to always do the right thing, and because I strived to set a track record that I and my family could be proud of.

Index

INDEX

INDEX

Record of Achievement

Olympic Champion
Olympic 200m Silver Medallist
World 100m Bronze Medallist
Three Time European Champion
Twice Commonwealth Games Champion
World Junior Champion
Double European Junior Champion

1991

European Junior Championships	1st	Gold Medal	100m
European Junior Championships	1st	Gold Medal	200m
European Junior Championships	2nd	Silver Medal	4 x 100m relay

1992

World Junior Championships	1st	Gold Medal	4 x 100m relay
World Junior Championships	2nd	Silver Medal	100m
World Junior Championships	2nd	Silver Medal	200m

1997

AAA (British Championships)	2nd	Silver Medal	100m
World Championships	3rd	Bronze Medal	4 x 100m relay

1998

AAA British Championships	1st	Gold Medal	100m
European Championships	1st	Gold Medal	100m
European Championships	1st	Gold Medal	4 x 100m relay
Commonwealth Games	1st	Gold Medal	4 x 100m relay

1999

AAA British Championship	3rd	Bronze Medal	100m
World Championships	2nd	Silver Medal	4 x 100m relay

2000

Olympic Games	2nd	Silver Medal	200m
AAA British Championships	1st	Gold Medal	100m
AAA British Championships	1st	Gold Medal	4 x 100m relay
Olympic Games		Finalist	100m

2002

AAA British Championshipships	2nd	Silver Medal	100m
European Championshipships	2nd	Silver Medal	100m
AAA British Championships	3rd	Bronze Medal	200m
Commonwealth Games	2nd	Silver Medal	200m
Commonwealth Games	1st	Gold Medal	4 x 100m relay

2003

AAA British Championships	1st	Gold Medal	100m
World Championships		Finalist	200m
World Championships	3rd	Bronze Medal	100m

2004

Olympic Games	1st	Gold Medal	4 x 100m relay
AAA British Championships	2nd	Silver Medal	100m
World Championships		Finalist	200m

2006

European Championships	1st	Gold Medal	4 x 100m relay